HYPNOSIS: *Theory, Practice and Application*

HYPNOSIS: *Theory, Practice and Application*

BY RAPHAEL H. RHODES

FOREWORD BY FOSTER KENNEDY, M.D.
Professor of Neurology, Cornell University College of Medicine; Director, Neurological Service Bellevue Hospital, New York

A Citadel Press Book
Published by Carol Publishing Group

A Citadel Press Book
Published by Carol Publishing Group
Citadel Press is a registered trademark of Carol Communications, Inc.

Editorial, sales and distribution, rights and permissions inquiries should be addressed to Carol Publishing Group, 120 Enterprise Avenue, Secaucus, N.J. 07094

In Canada: Canadian Manda Group, One Atlantic Avenue, Suite 105, Toronto, Ontario M6K 3E7

Carol Publishing Group books may be purchased in bulk at special discounts for sales promotions, fund-raising, or educational purposes. Special editions can be created to specifications. For details, contact Special Sales Department, Carol Publishing Group, 120 Enterprise Avenue, Secaucus, N.J. 07094

Manufactured in the United States of America
ISBN 0-8065-1119-2

25 24 23 22 21 20 19 18 17

This is an unaltered and unabridged republication of the first edition.

To My Wife

Foreword

Hypnosis has come a long way since the French Academy of Sciences denounced Mesmer's magnetism as fraud. Braid gave the practice its appropriate name, derived from the Greek word for sleep; and Bramwell, Forel, Munsterberg, Erickson, Lindner, Wm. Brown, Wolberg, and others endowed it with the substance of achievement in recorded cases.

Nevertheless physicians have been slow to embrace hypnosis as a therapeutic agent. Trained in a scientific mode of thought, they seek certainty: certainty of etiology and certainty of technique. In the realm of hypnosis, the search for certainty is still labyrinthine. Attempts to explain why it is effective run the gamut of psychological theories, from "suggestion" to conditioning through dissociation.

The literature of hypnotic practice is sparse on methodology, nor so far as I know, does any medical school offer a course in the technique of its induction.

This book advances a theory of hypnosis: the "Theory of Psychic Relative Exclusion," which purports to explain the *why* of hypnotism in terms which are also applicable to waking thought processes. This theory especially interests me because of its similarity to my own concept of hypnosis, of sleep, and of true hysterical sensory loss as being akin to the laying down of a radio curtain to block message transmission.

The chapters on hypnotic technique are detailed and helpful. I have watched the author use these methods, and have seen him achieve rapid hypnosis of patients whose previous experiences had led them to believe that they would be difficult to hypnotize. The variety of methods outlined for the induction of hypnotic sleep, and the specific suggestions for its therapeutic application, give this book really practical value.

FOSTER KENNEDY, M.D.

Preface

WHAT IS hypnosis? How is it induced? Why does it produce such astounding results? The physicians and psychologists who have done the most work in this field disagree among themselves in their answers to these questions.

To explain hypnosis, various hypotheses have been offered, a number of which I shall discuss in this book. Some theories of the nature of sleep have been propounded. Other theories have been evolved in an attempt to show why the Freudian psychoanalytic technique works. But there has been none comprehensive in scope; none which in, by, and through its own premises answers all of the questions and explains all of the issues arising from these phenomena.

In my quest for a solution of these problems, I have developed the theory presented in the following pages. The substance of it is based in part on material in T. J. Hudson's *Law of Psychic Phenomena,* first published in 1893; but Hudson's work is so replete with the unproved dogma of spiritualism and other supernatural matters that it is scientifically valueless. I have utilized only those of Hudson's ideas that appear to satisfy pragmatic tests. The explanation, in terms of the theory, of why Freud's psychoanalytic technique achieves its results, is wholly original with me.

RAPHAEL H. RHODES

New York City
September 11, 1950.

Acknowledgment

For the rare combination of discernment and imagination, patience and zeal, with which she served as critic and editor of this book, I gratefully acknowledge indebtedness to my wife, Irma Gelber Rhodes. I wish to express my appreciation, too, for Dr. William Menaker's kindness in reading the manuscript and for the many helpful suggestions he made.

R.H.R.

Contents

PART TWO

Hypnosis—Technique and Specific Application

9. Maintaining and Extending Hypnotic
      Control   91

10. Waking the Subject   115

11. Specific Application (Hints for the
       Practitioner)   124

12. Representative Cases   138

    Bibliography   149

    Index   169

PART ONE

Hypnosis—Theory and Application

Introduction

Hypnotism is the scientific key to mental control, the open sesame through which we reach the innermost recesses of thought. The hypnotist commands, "Sleep," and the subject slumbers. He suggests mirth and the subject laughs; or sorrow, and the subject cries. He demands sharpening of memory, and the long-obscured events of early childhood emerge from the nebulous shadows of the past to take form and substance once more.

In the middle of the nineteenth century, before the discovery of the anaesthetic properties of ether and chloroform, Dr. Esdaile in India performed over two hundred major operations and thousands of minor ones; yet not one of his patients suffered the

3

agony endured by other victims of the surgical procedure of that period. He employed hypnosis. His
subjects became oblivious to pain upon command.
J. M. Bramwell in his *Hypnotism, Its History, Practice and Theory* cites hundreds of interesting cases in
which cures were achieved through hypnosis. He
records, among others:

"A case of compound fracture of the leg, in which
a portion of the bone was sawn off, and the fracture
set during mesmeric trance. Several cases of strangulated hernia, which had resisted all attempts at re-
duction: during mesmeric sleep, there was complete
relaxation of the abdominal muscles; and in every
instance the hernia was easily reduced."

With the advent of drug-anaesthesia, interest in
hypnotism waned and its progress was arrested for
many years. The anaesthetics were quickly and easily
administered by the average physician, whereas hypnosis was still time-consuming and required a technique which only a minimal few had mastered.
Recently, however, in various types of operative
work, where drugs for anaesthesia have been deemed
inadvisable, hypnotism has been used successfully.
In childbirth, for example, it achieves painlessness
without destroying mother-cooperation, whereas
drugs numb both the mother's pain and her will to
work.

Hypnotism for anaesthesia has the further advantage that the insensitivity to pain may be continued

into the waking stage, by what is known as post-hypnotic suggestion; thus through this psychic form of anaesthesia the patient is enabled to enjoy the post-operative period of recovery free from the discomforts and dangers which otherwise may follow when a drug-anaesthesia wears off.

This phenomenon first attracted my attention several decades ago when, as an impressionable adolescent, I witnessed an operation in a dental surgeon's office. The dentist was cutting deeply into the patient's gum. The patient sat back, composed and comfortable, though no drug had been administered. She had merely been hypnotized. The hypnotist had told her to relax. He had said that she would feel no pain.

At the conclusion of the operation, which lasted about half an hour, the dentist laid his instruments aside, and nodded to the hypnotist. The latter then addressed the patient: "When I wake you, there will be no pain, no headache, no after-effects. You'll feel well and happy. Now when I count to ten, you'll wake up."

Upon the final count she opened her eyes and smiled. "When does he begin?" she asked.

"Why, he's finished!" the hypnotist replied.

"Impossible! I don't feel a thing!"

"Spit into the sink and you'll see the blood."

When she did so, incredulity changed to astonishment. But she was not the only one so affected. I was astounded to see her eat and enjoy a meal within the hour.

I resolved then and there that if hypnotism could do that, I would make every effort to master its secrets. The case history detailed in the following paragraphs exemplifies what can be wrought by such mastery. And this book, which has grown from the seed of my youthful determination, has as one of its purposes the communication of those secrets.

Some time ago a gentleman came to me in a state of great unhappiness, which he could neither understand nor overcome. He was a middle-aged bachelor in good health. There were no noticeable physical defects, nor were there any observable nervous mannerisms. He had no financial problems. Long in the service of the same substantial, nationally active corporation, he earned close to seventy-five hundred dollars per annum, and his position had the earmarks of permanency. Nevertheless, he suffered constant mental perturbation. Fearful of talking in company lest he mis-speak, he was just as mortified by his awkward silences. Psychically insecure in his situation, he was so avid for advancement that he was in a turmoil over his failure to gain rapid promotion. Anxious to excel, he was yet held back by feelings of inferiority and inadequacy. He was particularly uneasy about his relationship with his business superior, Mr. Moss, who seemed never to appreciate him at all.

I hypnotized him and employed a combination of

direct suggestion, dream induction and hypnoanalysis. After making general suggestions for improvement of attitude and loss of self-consciousness, I added that between the current visit and the next one, he would have a dream which would symbolize his relationship to Mr. Moss, and that he would report it to me, without remembering that I had made the suggestions.

At the next session he reported a dream, substantially as follows: "I was walking in the woods, down South somewhere, where I used to live in my childhood. I was much younger in the dream, and my sisters were with me. The place seemed familiar. I had known it as a child. We went somewhere, I think, but that's all I remember." Questioning revealed that his sisters were considerably older than he was. When I asked whether Moss appeared in the dream, he said, "No." He could not explain the dream, except to say that it reminded him of his childhood.

During the course of hypnotic treatment at this conference, I again suggested that before the following visit, he would have a dream which would symbolize the cause of his difficulties, particularly those with Moss. I repeated that without being aware of the source of the suggestions, he would disclose the dream to me.

When he called the following week, the dream he reported was practically the same as the former one. As before, Moss was not in it. Again, he could not explain it, except as a memory of his childhood. But to me the interpretation was by this time clear. The subconscious was attempting to say: "You asked for a symbolization of my trouble with Moss. There is no such problem. The real difficulty dates back to my childhood, and is bound up with my relationship to my sisters during that period of my life."

Analysis of early memories quickly revealed the subject's unhappy childhood, during which he was dominated by his sisters, particularly the eldest. Yet when I asked him whether he agreed with my conclusions, he was at first uncertain, saying, "My sister doesn't dominate me now; in fact she's dependent upon me for support." Before long, however, he added, "I wish I could get rid of her, just get her out of my mind!" With the expression of this longing came a flash of insight that illuminated both past and present for him. He began to understand the pervasive influence of his lifelong emotional dependence upon this woman. He came to realize that all his inferiority feelings and anxieties stemmed from that central subconscious sister-dependence, so deeply rooted in his childhood.

In a subsequent session, in response to a post-hypnotic suggestion that he would have a dream symbolizing his new understanding of himself and his relationship to people, he recounted: "I was in a house down South, and many people were there; my eldest sister was there too. I appeared to be my present age, though. My sister had her back to me. I knew it was she, but I didn't speak to her." When asked to associate this dream in the waking state, he merely reiterated its content.

He was then hypnotized and again asked to associate the dream. He said: "I just thought of another part of it. Suddenly I walked out of that house, stark naked, and just stood outside. Then I walked in again and I felt very good." Further analysis elicited the explanation that he enjoyed walking out "stark naked" because it was doing something of which his sister would have deeply disapproved, and he felt so "very good" because he had done it without considering her wishes.

I saw this man twice a week for six weeks. During these consultations he came to appreciate fully his former subconscious attitude toward his sisters, and how it had carried over into his relationship with others, particularly with his superior at his place of employment. With increased understanding of himself, anxiety yielded to assurance, fear to fortitude, and deviousness to directness. The inferiority complex disappeared, and for the first time in his life he began to feel invested with the dignity and power of self-assertive, independent manhood.

The employment of hypnotism made possible not only the general suggestions, but also the posthypnotic induction of relevant dreams. While the psychoanalyst, without hypnosis, must wait months or years until the subject in free association uncovers and reveals the critical incident, the hypnoanalyst may initiate a vastly more rapid recovery of pertinent buried memories through a variety of techniques, one of which is dream induction as here described.

The therapeutic application of hypnotism is most effective in the psychological domain. There are many types of mental aberration, which though within the broad border lines of sanity, cause psychic blocks and conflicts with tragic results to the people who suffer from them. These deviations manifest themselves not only in attitudes of thought and modes of action, but even in the development of apparently physical disorders although the patient is in fact organically sound. In this category fall the cases of functional paralysis and of hysterical deafness or blindness or aphonia in addition to such obvious neuroses as neurasthenia, anxieties, obsessions, compulsions, and phobias. The instances of social withdrawal, psychic collapse, and nonorganic physical incapacity which were labelled shellshock in World War I, and psychoneurosis in World War II, are all fertile fields for hypnotic treatment.

The employment of hypnotism in cases of this type is not new. Indeed, Mesmer and Charcot used it chiefly for various kinds of hysterical disorders. Bernheim, Liebeault and Janet in France, Bramwell and Braid in England, Forel in Switzerland and Moll in Germany, are among the better known of a large number of workers in various countries who utilized hypnotism for therapeutic purposes and left us detailed reports of their remarkably successful results.

Yet, though the powers of hypnotism have long been known and applied, its entire history has been overcast by obscurity and occultism. The credulous and the incredulous alike have brought upon it either unwarranted veneration or unmerited opprobrium, and both groups have contributed to its neglect by the scientific world. The average person even today looks upon hypnosis for psychotherapy as a Faustian probing of profundities at the cost of a soul.

A reading of the simple statement of the theory that is set forth in the following pages will not only readily dispel this unfortunate impression, but will also reveal why and how spectacular cures are effected through this science where somatic medicine has failed.

CHAPTER ONE

The Theory of Psychic Relative Exclusion

T HE THEORY is as follows:
1. Every person has two minds, the objective and the subjective. The objective is that which controls the senses: hearing, sight, taste, touch, and smell. The subjective mind is that which controls memory.

2. The objective mind is capable of both inductive and deductive reasoning. The subjective mind is capable of deductive reasoning only; it cannot reason inductively.

A. Inductive reasoning is the process by which, given divers particulars, one arrives at a generalization. For example, a physician observing a child who presents the following symptoms: runny nose, sneezing, coughing, watering eyes, temperature of 101 degrees, bluish-white spots on the gums and a rash on the face and body, concludes from these particulars that this patient has the measles. The diagnosis is a generalization, arrived at by means of inductive reasoning.

B. Deductive reasoning is the process by which, given a generalization, one infers the particulars. To illustrate, I shall assume that the mother of the child in the example just cited reports to his teacher, "John is sick with the measles." The teacher may deduce the particulars: that her pupil has symptoms including runny nose, sneezing, coughing, watering eyes, a rise in temperature, spots on the gums, and a rash on the face and body.

The foregoing examples must, of course, be considered in the light of the impossibility of characterizing anything as a "particular" or a "generalization" for all purposes. The particulars in A lead to the generalization, "This patient has the measles," which is similar to the generalization in B, "John is sick with the measles." The generalization in B might, however, be a particular under other circumstances. For example, given the particulars: John is sick with the measles, one-third of his classmates in the district school have the measles, half of the children on his block are down with the measles; one arrives at the generalization that there is an epidemic of measles in John's neighborhood. Thus, what was a generalization in B, "John is sick with the measles," has now become a mere particular under the circumstances outlined in the preceding sentence.

The process is interminable, for every generalization may be utilized as a particular under other circumstances. However, this variability characteristic of any possible example of a particular or a generalization does not detract from the distinction between the logical processes by which, under a given set of circumstances, the particulars on the one hand or the generalizations on the other hand are arrived at.

Always, generalizations are arrived at through the inductive process, and particulars through the deductive. The objective mind is capable of both; the subjective mind, of the latter only.

The objective mind can do both A and B. The subjective mind can do B, but not A. The subjective mind reasons perfectly when only the deductive process is involved, but not at all when the inductive process is demanded.

In consequence of this limitation, the subjective mind accepts as true any generalization which is given to it, because, being incapable of the inductive process, it has no way of challenging that generalization. The only way of combatting a generalization is by arriving at a contrary one upon the basis of particulars noted; but that involves the inductive process, of which the subjective mind is not capable.

3. These two minds are ever present in each individual, in a relative state of seesaw balance. Neither is ever completely obliterated. As one comes to the fore, the other recedes; like the two ends of a seesaw, they supplement each other.

I have spoken of "two minds." The reader may, however, prefer to view the aggregate of the mental powers of each individual as the result of one entity, one mind. If so, that is permissible.

The content and validity of the theory remain unaltered in the face of a "one mind" concept, for in that event it merely becomes necessary to view the subjective and the objective as distinct phases of that one mind. The theory would then be expressed in terms of one mind having two distinct factors: the subjective factor and the objective factor. This would in no way affect the basic substance and application of the theory. It would merely involve a substitution of the terms employed.

As the subjective and the objective are distinct, one from the other, each possessing different powers and manifesting itself in its own unique way, I believe clarity of thought is served by viewing them as two separate minds, in order the better to distinguish between them. I have therefore elected to speak of the "subjective mind" and the "objective mind" as if they were separate entities.

Utilizing the words *objective, subjective, inductive* and *deductive* as words of art, with the meanings above described, we may epitomize the theory in the three numbered sentences:

1. Every person has two minds, the objective and the subjective.

2. The objective mind is capable of both inductive and deductive reasoning, but the subjective is capable of deductive reasoning only.

3. These two minds are ever present in each individual, in a relative state of seesaw balance.

This is the entire theory. I advance it because it is the simplest, and at the same time, the most comprehensive explanation of all psychological phenomena manifested by individuals while awake, asleep, or hypnotized.

Because the coming to the fore of one of these minds excludes the processes of the other to a concomitantly relative degree, I call this the Theory of Psychic Relative Exclusion. And when once the theory is understood, it may readily be applied to the alleviation and cure of numerous functional disorders and neurotic disturbances which have failed to yield to other forms of treatment.

Disorders of an apparently physical nature are organic or functional: organic when there is an impaired or destroyed physical organ, e.g. fractured or amputated limb, diseased or destroyed nerve cells, carcinoma, myopia, etc.; functional when the disorder is nonorganic in origin, e.g. hysterical blindness, aphasia, amnesia, paralysis, distortion or failure of taste or smell, etc., following psychic trauma or repression. Neurotic disturbances such as stuttering, anxieties, phobias, depressions, obsessions and hallucinations, and harmful habits such as excessive masturbation, chain-smoking, and intemperate drinking result sometimes from a specific mental shock or repression, but they are often traceable to less clearly delimitable causes like maladjustment due to unpleasant environmental factors.

Functional disorders and such neurotic disturbances, being entirely psychic in nature, are amenable to cure entirely through nonsomatic means. Physiology is apparently not involved.

CHAPTER TWO

General Application of the Theory

THE THEORY set forth in the preceding chapter supplies a simple and inclusive explanation for all the mental activity of persons, whether awake, asleep, or hypnotized.

The reader can readily apply the theory to a person who is awake. Since the objective mind is in control, sensory activity is strong. Utilization of the senses keeps the objective mind to the fore, and the subjective is then correspondingly recessive. Because of this temporarily recessive state of the subjective, memory is poor during periods of active use of the senses. Stimulation of recall is achieved by relaxing the objective interests, for as the objective mind withdraws, the subjective mind, controlling memory, advances. The more the objective interests are cast off, the more does the subjective come to the fore with consequent improvement of memory. That is why a person in the hypnotized state, during which the subjective mind is at the helm, has power of recall to an unusual degree.

During the waking state, with the objective mind in control, the individual is capable of both inductive and deductive reasoning; at the same time the recessive subjective mind is still sufficiently active for ordinary memory requirements. Logic pervades the reasoning processes and the individual's conclusions are normal. Any fantastic or abnormal idea is immediately rejected and dispelled, for the objective mind, reasoning inductively, arrives at logical (normal) generalizations upon the basis of observed particulars.

And now to invade the poet's realm—sleep and perchance dreams. "Care-charmer Sleep, son of the sable Night," "Sleep that knits up the ravell'd sleave of care," "Nature's soft nurse . . . that giv'st what Life denies"—is to the scientist simply a transposition of the phases of the waking mind. (How much more expansive the literary fields wherein one's imagination may freely roam, where equipped with poetic license one may ignore the traffic lights of logic!)

Ordinary sleep is achieved through a gradual recession of the objective. One thinks of nothing, allowing the senses to subside. When the senses have dulled sufficiently (i.e. the objective has become sufficiently recessive), the individual is asleep. As the objective recedes, the subjective advances.

When the individual sleeps, the subjective mind controls. That is why dreams are sometimes so queer.

A fantastic or abnormal idea is rejected and dispelled in the waking state through the inductive processes of the objective mind. That same idea, no matter how fantastic or abnormal, when conceived by the recessive objective while the individual sleeps, is transmitted to the dominant subjective and is accepted as true. It is accepted as a true generalization, for the subjective mind, incapable of inductive reasoning, has no way of questioning or combatting it.

Thus the idea that one is dead and at the same time attending his own funeral, which would be promptly rejected in the waking state, is a type of dream that is not uncommon. The absurdity of the idea is not apparent to the subjective mind, for the observed and known particulars which might lead to the contra-generalization of absurdity cannot lead to this result except through the inductive process, of which the subjective mind, in control of the sleeping individual, is incapable.

The reason why dreams are often wish-fulfillments also becomes clear. The desire, impossible of achievement in the face of merciless reality, becomes an accepted generalization when the inductive process is excluded.

Thus the theory redeems its prosy features by accounting for the most enchanting part of our slumbers, the dreams in which we enjoy the otherwise unattainable. The spirits of the night, genii of heaven's magic lanterns, are ours to command. The yacht we viewed with envy from our barren shore is ours to sail the seven seas upon. The unrequited love is fulfilled. The stammerer becomes an orator; the pedant, a wit; the lawyer, a politician; the politician, a statesman. Wishes become horses and beggars then ride.

So also daydreams, youth's highroad, and reveries, the byroad of age, are flights of the subjective mind, unfettered by the inductive processes of the objective in repose.

The theory also explains the phenomena of hypnotism. Hypnotic sleep differs from ordinary sleep in that it is induced by the hypnotist. The process depends upon the scientific application of methods and techniques within the boundaries of the Theory of Psychic Relative Exclusion as here set forth. The common impression that supernatural power is demanded is based upon ignorance and is wholly unfounded.

To secure hypnotic sleep, the hypnotist induces the objective mind of the subject to recede, thus bringing the subjective mind to the fore. But instead of coming to the fore as in ordinary sleep, without being controlled by, or subject to, any other mind, it comes to the fore with the expectation of being controlled by, and subject to, the suggestions of the hypnotist. This expectation of the subjective mind is in the nature of an accepted generalization, and this explains the hypnotist's resultant control.

Autohypnosis is a variant condition in which the subjective advances with the expectation of being controlled by the subject's own objective mind.

Hypnosis may be defined as a condition in which a shift in the relative positions of the subjective and objective minds has been consummated, and in which the subjective has been brought to the fore with the expectation of being controlled either by the hypnotist or by the recessive objective. The process which achieves this result is hypnotism. When it is induced by a hypnotist, and the subjective advances with the expectation of being controlled by the hypnotist, it is called hypnotism by external control. When the subject himself induces the subjective-objective shift, and the subjective advances with the expectation of being controlled by the recessive objective, the process is called autohypnotism or autohypnosis.

The topic of autohypnosis is treated in a separate chapter. The present chapter deals only with hypnotism by external control.

Once a subject has been hypnotized by external control, he becomes subject to and is controlled by the suggestions thereafter made by the hypnotist. This follows from the fact that in the process of being hypnotized, his subjective mind has advanced with the expectation of such control, and this expectation of control by the hypnotist is in the nature of a subjectively accepted generalization. Thus the subjective mind, which is in direct control of the subject, in turn accepts the hypnotist's suggestions as its motivating media.

The control, once established, may be maintained and extended at the will of the hypnotist; for once the subject's subjective mind accepts the hypnotist as its source of suggestions, any suggestion thereafter made by the hypnotist assumes for the subject the nature of an incontrovertible generalization.

Even an anaesthetic effect may be achieved, without drugs, by the use of hypnotic suggestion alone. Such anaesthesia, which upon superficial consideration appears to be a sensory and therefore an objective factor, is obtained through control of the subjective when the latter is to the fore, because the suggestion, accepted by the dominant subjective, rules the subject's mind to the extent that it will refuse to recognize any nerve impulses which ordinarily would lead to a contra-generalization. The nerve messages which would normally register as a sensation of pain are particulars which the subjective refuses to recognize when they are inconsonant with the already accepted generalization of anaesthesia.

Control, after it has been assumed, may be maintained or extended by the mere suggestion of its con-

tinuance or extension, for the suggestion of maintenance or extension is accepted by the subjective as
a true generalization.

The degree of hypnotic control at any particular
moment depends upon the extent to which the objective mind of the subject has been made to recede,
or putting it conversely, the extent to which the
subject's subjective mind has been brought to the
fore.

The extent of control is not unlimited. It is circumscribed by the degree to which the objective mind of
the subject, though recessive, is still present. That is
why, no matter how successful the hypnosis may be,
it is impossible to overcome certain basic instincts
and deeply ingrained tenets of the subject. Just what
such instincts and tenets are, varies among different
individuals. Most persons have a basic instinct for
self-preservation. Among women, chastity before,
and fidelity in marriage are deeply ingrained tenets
for a large percentage. The same is true of religious
beliefs, which are often too firmly rooted to yield to
countersuggestion during hypnosis. Similarly certain
other moral, ethical, and spiritual values assume
significant proportions for many persons, but the
degree is an individual matter.

Relinquishment of control may be positive or
negative. It is usually positive: the hypnotist suggests that upon a given signal the subject will awake.
The suggestion is effective because the subjective

mind of the subject accepts it like any other generalization, and thereupon at the given signal it accordingly recedes, allowing the objective to come to the fore. Negative relinquishment of control would follow from an extended absence of any suggestions from the hypnotist, in consequence of which the objective mind of the subject would gradually advance and the subjective would correspondingly recede: in effect the subject would pass into a state of natural sleep and then awaken therefrom.

Aside from the hypnotist's control of the subject through the latter's responses to specific suggestions while in the hypnotic state, there are two other possible consequences:

1. Utilization of the subject's increased power of recall during the hypnotic state; and

2. Implantation of suggestions in the subject's subjective mind, with continuing (posthypnotic) effect.

These two are the bases of psychotherapy through hypnotic control.

CHAPTER THREE

Therapeutic Application
(External Control)

H YPNOSIS is an effective aid in various kinds of psychotherapeutic work. Two approaches are possible, and either or both may be used in any particular case: (1) Utilization of the increased memory ability of the subject during the hypnotic state, and (2) Possible implantation of suggestions in the subject's subjective mind, with continuing (posthypnotic) effect.

As previously stated, these are the bases of psychotherapy through hypnotic control. This is true whether the hypnotic control is external or self-induced. The present chapter deals with aspects of external control (i.e. by a hypnotist upon the subject) and the following chapter will be devoted to aspects of self-induced control (i.e. by the subject upon himself).

INCREASED MEMORY

A person's ability to recall past events correctly is almost always greater in the hypnotic state than it is when that person is awake. This increased recall ability is termed *hypermnesia*.

Hypermnesia in the hypnotic state is wholly consonant with the Theory of Psychic Relative Exclusion, in that the subjective mind (controlling memory) comes to the fore as the objective recedes. For the same reason the theory also explains the common experience of increased memory facility in the waking state upon relaxation and suppression of current objective interests.

In practically all psychotherapeutic work, and especially where the Freudian psychoanalytic technique is employed, recall of long past events, previous mental reactions to long past events, and conscious realization of the thought pattern resulting therefrom, are often demanded.

For simplicity of expression I will hereafter use the term "crucial incident" to designate all such repressed past events, previous reactions to them, and thought patterns resulting therefrom (i.e. repressed memories and unconscious strivings) which have caused functional disorder or neurotic disturbance.

Any approach to uncovering such crucial incidents with the subject in the waking state usually involves lengthy sessions in which the subject is urged to "talk himself out" to the psychologist or psychoanalyst, who attempts thus to elicit the desired information. In most cases, even when the subject finally recalls and relates the crucial incident, he is not personally aware of its significance until the psychologist or psychoanalyst indicates and explains it to him. Generally, when the crucial incident has been uncovered and its significance explained and understood, the functional disorder or neurosis which it produced will disappear. (Of course, rehabilitation and reorientation processes are also necessary in appropriate cases, but these must follow the uncovering of the crucial incident.)

Hypnotically induced hypermnesia will generally produce the desired recall much more expeditiously than is possible in the waking state. Pragmatically, this method has demonstrated its worth; it results in much more rapid recall of the desired crucial incident, and in a quicker appreciation of its significance by the subject.

The method, once hypnotic control is established, is, in a large percentage of cases, superior to and simpler than the ordinary psychoanalytic technique; superior in its rapidity in achieving results, and simpler by virtue of this rapidity, resulting in a directness in attaining the desired goal, which eliminates otherwise complicating bypaths.

The conversational technique employed is similar to that used in non-hypnotic analysis. The method differs chiefly in that hypnotic control is first established, and in that (once the subject is asleep) control is extended at first through short questions and answers to confirm sleeping conversational facility. (Even in the waking state, a certain amount of preliminary two-way conversation is required before conversational ease is attained and established by the subject.) A procedure which sometimes brings about a gratifying result is to suggest to the hypnotized subject that he retell each of the instances when the disorder complained of manifested itself. He sometimes recalls these instances in receding memorial stages, finally going back to the first one, which often is at the time of, or very close to, the desired crucial incident.

A verbatim report of the hypnoanalysis of a criminal psychopath is to be found in *Rebel Without a Cause* by Robert M. Lindner, published in 1944 by Grune and Stratton. Lindner suggests preliminary psychoanalytic conversation in the waking state, followed by the use of hypnosis to evoke the crucial incident. This method has the advantage (among others) that it may be utilized by psychoanalysts who themselves may be poor or untrained hypnotists, for the hypnosis may be induced by a hypnotist other than the analyst; and the questioning of the subject in the hypnotic state may be either by such hypnotist in the analyst's presence, or even by the analyst himself after the hypnotist has made the appropriate suggestions to the subject.

The superiority of the hypnotic method of inducing hypermnesia is explained theoretically: (1) by the coming to the fore of the subjective mind (which controls memory), and (2) by the fact that the repressed crucial incidents (whether events or reactions to events or thought patterns) which are causing the functional disorders are apparently lodged in the subjective mind in the nature of unrecalled memory factors.

The second point, i.e. that the repressed or unconscious disturbing crucial incidents are lodged in the subjective mind as unrecalled memory factors, is important to the theory here expounded and to the practice advocated. While repressed and causing functional disorders or neuroses, these crucial incidents are *not* part of the objective (current, conscious) mind; when they become part of the objective mind, the functional disorder or neurosis disappears. The disability endures, however, as long as the crucial incident is a factor of the subjective mind alone, i.e. an incident which has become part of the subject's memory pattern, unrecalled.

Events recalled in the trance state appear in one of two memory types: either *revivified* or *regressive*.

Where an event is recalled in its original state, without regard or relation to subsequently occurring events or subsequently acquired knowledge or attitudes of the subject, the recalled experience is termed *revivified:* the past event, *as such,* is revivified. Where, however, the recall appears in the light of, and in relation to, the knowledge and attitudes acquired by the subject since the occurrence of the recalled event, the recalled experience is termed *regressive.* A revivified memory is generally revealed by the subject's reliving the past event in the attitude which prevailed with him at the time the event first occurred. A regressive memory, on the other hand, will probably be revealed coupled with an expression of attitude or judgment based upon the knowledge of the subject acquired between the time of the original occurrence and the time of the revelation.

The difference between these memory types depends upon the extent to which, and the length of time during which, the incident or event remembered has been lodged in the subjective mind alone. An incident or event which has been lodged in the subjective alone from the time of its happening (or very shortly thereafter) until its recall and revelation, will be revealed in its original state, without relation to subsequently acquired knowledge and attitudes of the objective. It will be a revivified memory. If, on the other hand, the event or incident has been recalled from time to time between its original occurrence and the ultimate revelation, it will be revealed subject to and colored by the subject's objective knowledge and attitudes acquired since its inception. The same is true where recall is not immediately followed by revelation, and where the revelation comes only after objective consideration of the recalled experience. In both of the latter instances, the memory is revealed as regressive.

In inducing hypnotic sleep, the operator brings the subject's subjective mind to the fore. This is that part of the subject's mind in which alone is lodged the desired crucial incident. In the hypnotic condition the subject more readily recalls the desired crucial incident, not only because the subjective mind controls memory, but furthermore because, relieved of the repressing influence of the objective mind, the subjective is free to recall the crucial incident in its original state, uninfluenced and undistorted by the normally repressing interests and attitudes of the subject's waking objective mind. Thus through hypnosis the crucial incident is more quickly revealed in its original state and perspective than is possible when the subject is awake and consequently confused by his objective (current, conscious) preoccupations.

It is interesting to note that the theory here propounded explains not only the results achieved through hypnotic control—as well as ordinary sleep and the thinking processes in the waking state—but also, what to my mind has never been satisfactorily explained before, to wit: the reason *why* the Freudian psychoanalytic technique works, that is, why functional disorders or neuroses disappear when the crucial incident is uncovered and its significance explained and understood.

This explanation is based upon the inability of the subjective mind to reason inductively. The objective mind, which is capable of both inductive and deductive reasoning, quickly dispels the functional disorder or neurosis once it is aware of and understands the significance of the crucial incident; because, utilizing the inductive process, and treating the crucial incident as merely one particular together with all other particulars of which it is cognizant, it relegates the crucial incident to a position of proper relationship in conjunction with the other particulars, and arrives at normal generalizations upon the basis of all of the particulars known to it. All of its generalizations are thereupon normal; the abnormal generalization which produced the functional disorder or neurosis is dispelled and the abnormal manifestation disappears.

The former inability of the subjective mind alone to accomplish this result is best understood by considering how the functional disorder arose in the first instance. An incident, generally extremely unpleasant or simultaneous with shock, is rejected by the objective (current, conscious) mind of the subject so completely that it lodges in the subjective (memory) mind alone. Because of its sudden, forceful, and unique rejection by the objective, it lodges in the subjective mind, detached and isolated from the other particulars with which the objective would normally associate it. Thus isolated and detached from other normalizing particulars, it becomes to the subjective mind either in itself or through itself the cause of an accepted *abnormal* generalization which the subjective alone cannot counteract since it is incapable of inductive reasoning; and this accepted abnormal generalization results in abnormal conduct which manifests itself as a functional disorder or a neurosis. This accepted, abnormal generalization, lodged in the subjective mind where it is impervious to inductive attack, remains rigid and inflexible; and the drives it engenders manifest pervasive effects, unimpeded by the usual normalizing factor of conscious thought.

This functional disorder or neurosis persists as long as the accepted abnormal generalization remains. It remains as long as it is lodged in the subjective alone. Being lodged there, disassociated and isolated from other particulars which have not been so suddenly, forcefully, and uniquely rejected and repressed by the objective mind, it is not ordinarily recalled in any usual way, but only as the result of extraordinary probing. This extraordinary probing is

generally accomplished by the Freudian psychoanalytic technique. It may be accomplished more
expeditiously through hypnotic control, i.e. hypnoanalysis. Once the crucial incident is thus uncovered
and its significance explained and understood by the
objective mind, the inductive process arrives at normal generalizations as above explained and the dis·
order disappears.

Freud himself at first used, but soon discarded,
hypnotism, and he did not advocate it for psychoanalytic work. I believe the reason for his lack of
enthusiasm for the hypnotic medium inhered in the
fact that the method he employed in securing hypnotic control was undeveloped, and ordinarily con-
sumed anywhere from twenty minutes to a greater
length of time in each instance. The cumbersome
hypnotic technique employed by him is outmoded
and the need for it obviated by the methods in current use, the more rapid of which have been developed in recent years. Freud's distrust of hypnosis
may also have been based upon the fact that, at the
time he abandoned it, he had not yet developed the
technique of free association. Hypnotism therefore
appeared to him to be merely a complete domination
of the subject by the hypnotist. But today, in the
light of our understanding of the principles of free
association, thanks to Freud's arduous and fruitful
endeavors, we are ready to take the next step, to
utilize the hypnotic technique to supplement and

thereby enhance the value of orthodox psycho-analysis.

Freud recognized the usefulness of hypnotism to induce hypermnesia; he recorded in his *Autobiographical Study* that ". . . hypnotism had been of immense help in the cathartic treatment, by widening the field of the patient's consciousness and putting within his reach knowledge which he did not possess in his waking life."

One special caution is necessary when using hypnosis to induce hypermnesia for psychotherapy, namely: that the operator carefully avoid making any suggestion as to the nature of the crucial incident. Such a suggestion might be accepted by the subject; whereas the desired result, on the contrary, is that the subject himself actually recall and uncover the true crucial incident which underlies his disorder.

Posthypnotic Suggestion

The use of posthypnotic suggestion alone, where preliminary analysis is called for, will remove the symptoms only, but not their cause. In all such cases, therefore, hypnoanalysis is to be preferred.

Sometimes, however, the psychoanalytic method, even with the help of hypnotic control, is unavailing or uncalled for. This may be due (1) to the fact that the functional disorder or neurosis attacked is based upon a crucial incident which is extremely difficult to uncover; or (2) to the fact that the crucial incident which was the original factor in causing the disorder has since been supplanted by other factors (e.g. acquired habits or reflexes, social relationships or attitudes) as current substitute cause of the disorder; or (3) to the fact that there is no crucial incident underlying the disorder.

In cases of the third type the problem is generally not one of eliminating a functional disorder, but rather that of eliminating some undesirable behavior pattern (generally based upon instinctive or acquired social attitudes), or adjusting mental reactions to persons, things, and events. These problems may have no relationship to any particular crucial incident. For example, shyness manifesting itself in asocial behavior, may in many cases result from general environmental factors (such as the lack of proper attention in the home during the formative years, or overshadowing because of the superiority of other members of the family), or from the necessity of complying with a mode of living distasteful to the subject (such as wearing eyeglasses or a hearing device). The resulting undesirable behavior pattern in such a case is not caused by any particular crucial incident; not only is there no crucial incident to uncover and explain, but on the contrary the cause of the difficulty has probably been known to the subject all along, and the consequent disorder or behavior pattern is a reaction which to him seems logical and natural. It is therefore difficult, if not impossible, to overcome this kind of behavior through ordinary psychoanalytic or argumentative means.

The same is true of reactions to persons, things and events which, although not manifesting themselves in functional disorders or undesirable behavior patterns, do cause irritation, annoyance, dissatisfaction or unpleasantness to the subject, whether mental or physical, or both. For example, a person who must wear a hearing device on account of an impairment of the aural organs, although he may not in consequence thereof manifest any functional disorder or any undesirable behavior pattern, may nevertheless be continually irritated, annoyed, dissatisfied and unhappy because of it. This reaction may result from an aversion to having the physical defect made so conspicuous, or from the physical annoyance occasioned by the wearing of the apparatus, or both. Among other things, such hearing devices often disturb the wearer by amplifying and transmitting unwanted sounds (e.g. the swish of the wearer's clothing in movement against the microphone is amplified and transmitted directly to the ear with continually disturbing effect). In such instances the psychoanalytic technique is uncalled for.

In cases where (1) the crucial incident is extremely hard to uncover or (2) other factors have supplanted the original crucial incident as current substitute cause of the disorder, the psychoanalytic technique may be unavailing: not because its application is impossible, but because the necessary length of treatment in such cases may be irreconcilable with the intellectual or financial limitations of the subject.

Most of the disorders and disturbances in which the psychoanalytic technique is either unavailing or uncalled for may be alleviated or cured through posthypnotic suggestion.

By posthypnotic suggestion is meant a therapeutic suggestion or suggestions made directly to the subjective mind of a subject who is in a state of hypnotic trance, with the added suggestion that it will have continuing (posthypnotic) effect even after the subject is awakened. The therapeutic suggestions and the suggestion of continuity are both accepted by the subject's subjective mind as true generalizations, and as such become part of his accepted and natural thought pattern. The suggestions are perforce accepted as true generalizations by the subjective mind because of its inability to reason inductively.

Having thus become part of the subject's thought pattern, and remaining such even in the waking state, the therapeutic suggestions control his waking thought pattern and thus influence his subsequent waking behavior.

The reason why these suggestions have continuing (posthypnotic) effect is that the subjective mind accepts as true generalizations not only the therapeutic suggestions, but also the suggestion of continuance;

thus even after the subject is awakened, his subjective mind expects a carry-through of the therapeutic suggestions, and influences the objective mind (then in control) to conform to this expectation.

At this point there is a conflict between the accustomed thoughts and actions of the subject, and the thought patterns and actions demanded by the subjective. It is for this reason that posthypnotic suggestions do not necessarily achieve the desired results in one session. The influence may be only partial at first, but repetition gives it gradually increasing force, like repeated impulses to a pendulum or a freely revolving wheel.

Similar suggestions with like influence may be made without any hypnosis, but their effect will be inconsiderable when compared with the force of the suggestions made when the subject is in the hypnotic state, because in the latter case they are made directly to the subjective mind.

The therapeutic suggestions and the suggestion of continuity may be coupled with the suggestion of amnesia as to the source of the impulses, in order to achieve effective results more quickly. When the subject awakes, if he is not consciously aware of the fact that a posthypnotic suggestion has been given, he is less able to counteract its effect. When he is conscious of the exact nature of the posthypnotic suggestion, the awakened subject more easily combats the impulses; sometimes to such a degree that the mere knowledge that a particular posthypnotic suggestion has been made may be sufficient to nullify its effect. On the other hand, if their origin is forgotten, the impulses strike him with an apparently natural force which he accepts unquestioningly and acts upon more willingly, as one naturally follows through with better grace an idea or plan which is one's own rather than that of another. Such posthypnotic suggestions exert a strong influence. When their source remains unknown to the subject, they have a pervasive force similar to that of unresolved subconscious drives.

Of course, in therapeutic work it is presupposed that the subject has requested the treatment. In this type of work, therefore, the subject will generally be aware of the fact that posthypnotic suggestions are being made, though posthypnotic amnesia may render him unaware of their specific content; and, furthermore, even when the subject is aware of the specific content of the posthypnotic suggestions made, his over-all desire to achieve a cure will reduce the amount of objective countersuggestion.

No constant formula can be devised with regard to the extent to which amnesia should be suggested as a concomitant of posthypnotic suggestion. The psychologist varies his method from case to case, keeping in mind all of the foregoing factors.

Where possible, it is helpful to have the subject enact the posthypnotic suggestion while still in the sleeping state; kinaesthesia helps to reinforce the memory and will be conducive to a stronger implantation of the thought pattern in the subjective mind. The enactment in the sleeping state is followed by suggestion that the same will remain true even after the subject is awake.

The method of making posthypnotic suggestions may be illustrated, for example, with a person who desires to overcome the cigarette smoking habit. With the subject in hypnotic trance, ask whether he desires a cigarette. When he answers affirmatively, say, "When I give you this cigarette, you'll light it, and take deep puffs. The first puff will be slightly bitter; the second puff more bitter; the third puff will be very bitter and acrid—you won't like it at all; the fourth puff will be so bitter and acrid that you'll spit —it will be very, very distasteful; the fifth puff will taste worse than any of the others—you'll positively hate it, you'll throw the cigarette away."

The suggestion is followed by enactment in the sleeping state. Then ask, "Didn't you like it?" Later, "That's what will happen every time you smoke a cigarette. Even after I wake you up, it will always happen the same way; the first puff will be bitter and the next even worse, and after a few puffs you'll have a terrible taste in your mouth and you'll throw the cigarette away. You'll get to dislike smoking. During the next week you'll start only ten cigarettes a day— not more, maybe fewer, and they'll taste worse and worse. You won't remember that I was the one who told this to you; but it will work that way, naturally, by itself, just as I said."

Posthypnotic suggestion may also be utilized to make a person oblivious to otherwise irritating or annoying factors. For example, dislike of a hearing aid because of its conspicuousness may be attacked as follows: "You are now using the hearing device and you're not uncomfortable or self-conscious because of it." (This assumes prior suggestions which overcame the discomfort and self-consciousness.) "Now when I wake you up, you won't be any more uncomfortable or self-conscious about it than you are now. You'll continue to be perfectly at ease, comfortable and quite unself-conscious when using the device. The more you use it, the more will you get to feel that it is natural and not at all conspicuous. You won't remember that I was the one who told this to you, but it will work that way, naturally, by itself, just as I said."

In some cases the posthypnotic suggestion may even be able to eliminate irritating pressure or sound. A person may be made oblivious to the pressure of the hearing device against his person, or to the buzz occasioned by the swish of his clothing against the microphone as he moves. This specific oblivion is first established in the sleeping state, and then carried through into the waking state. The establishment of the specific oblivion does not affect or impair the subject's senses to anything other than the specific object attacked; you can make sure of this by including a suggestion to this effect.

Posthypnotic suggestion is also used by psychoanalysts in appropriate cases to establish, foster, renew—or when necessary, destroy—the transference between analyst and subject. (The destruction of transference is one of the most complex of psychoanalytic problems, and posthypnotic suggestion for this purpose should be used only in the rarest instances.)

The types of cases for which posthypnotic suggestion may be helpful are legion. A few may be indicated:

Insomnia
Disturbing dreams and nightmares
Somnambulism
Overanxiety
Fears and phobias: claustrophobia, acrophobia, gynophobia, xenophobia, etc. Fear of thunderstorms, lightning, earthquakes, etc.
Morbidity
Hypochondria
Compulsions
Obsessions
Depressions
Hallucinations
Delusions

Sadism

Masochism

Narcissism

Abnormal sexual indulgence, excessive masturbation or functional sexual disability

Neurotic disturbance accompanying menopause, or following miscarriage or childbirth

Amnesia

Functional paralysis, blindness, aphonia and deafness

Functional hypertension

Functional speech disorders (most types of stuttering or vocal hesitancy)

Nervous headache

Nervous habits including twitches, tics and contractures; nailbiting; excessive smoking, drinking and eating

Self-consciousness or shyness due to physical defects, such as loss of limb, scars, deafness, blemishes, etc.

Personality defects: shyness, pugnacity, temper, awkwardness, dependency

Habitual prevarication

Kleptomania and some other criminal or antisocial tendencies

Drug addiction

Some of these disorders which are particularly characteristic of youthful and adolescent phases are an especially fertile field for posthypnotic suggestion.

Many persons who have no functional or neurotic complaint may nevertheless benefit from certain types of posthypnotic suggestion. For example, the public performer—singer, instrumentalist, actor, speaker, etc.—may thus achieve a revamping of personality factors, and control of voice and manner, resulting in increased audience rapport. In the same way the lawyer, the engineer, the executive, or the salesman may gain the benefits of accomplished assurance, poise and persuasiveness.

In many instances where the application of somatic medicine is unavailing, psychotherapy through hypnotic control may achieve the desired cure. In his work on *Office Treatment of Nose, Throat, and Ear,* A. R. Hollender says with reference to hysterical aphonia, on page 390:

"For patients who will not respond to suggestion, Clerf recommends hypnosis, claiming that most persons with functional aphonia are susceptible to this measure. . . . Clerf believes that there are dangers of 'fixing the neurosis' by protracted medication and instrumentation. Attention is directed to the fact that mere removal of the superficial symptoms does not mean that the patient is cured. Usually the only result of treatment by electricity and gadgets is changing the locus of the complaint. . . ."

The degree to which a subject may be cured by posthypnotic suggestion alone, sufficiently to become independent of the hypnotist, varies from case to case. The dependence on the hypnotist is gradually decreased in the course of treatment so that less and less suggestion is necessary, and longer and longer intervals between the sessions are established. The influence of the subjective upon the objective, acting with gradually increasing impact, finally produces an objective stability based upon the new thought pattern, which by replacement eliminates the formerly objectionable behavior or reaction. This is the result in a majority of cases.

There is, however, a minority which seems to remain dependent. In such cases the therapist may consider teaching the subject autohypnosis, which is discussed in the following chapter.

CHAPTER FOUR

Therapeutic Application
(SELF-INDUCED CONTROL: AUTOHYPNOSIS)

ALTHOUGH there is a large literature dealing with autosuggestion in the waking state (made popular by Coué), the subject of scientific autohypnosis is comparatively young. Developed within this decade by Andrew Salter, a psychologist, its principles and methods were detailed in his article entitled "Three Techniques of Autohypnosis," which appeared first in the April 1941 edition of *The Journal of General Psychology* and again in 1944 as an appendix to his book entitled *What Is Hypnosis.* "Three Techniques of Autohypnosis" is a valuable contribution toward the advance of the science of hypnotism, and I cannot do better than to commend it to those interested in this phase of the subject. The article sets forth three modes by which a subject may be taught to hypnotize himself, that is to put himself into a trance, to give himself suggestions which have posthypnotic effect, and then to awaken himself.

The Theory of Psychic Relative Exclusion furnishes the theoretical explanation for autohypnosis by the fact that the subjective and the objective are always present in each individual in a relative state of seesaw balance, so that the objective is never wholly obliterated in the hypnotic state, but only recessive. Autohypnosis is accomplished through the subject's learning how to bring his subjective to the fore while accomplishing simultaneously the recession of the objective, yet retaining the latter in sufficient degree as the positive source of suggestions purposefully planned and given. These are readily accepted by the subjective, not only because of its inability to reject generalizations, but furthermore because it comes to the fore with the expectation of accepting (being controlled by) the subject's consciously made suggestions (objectively propelled thoughts).

The techniques of autohypnosis as developed by Salter enable a subject to become independent of the hypnotist in all cases where the psychotherapeutic result may be achieved through posthypnotic suggestion. The same is not necessarily true of cures which depend upon the uncovering of a crucial incident; in such cases the psychoanalytic technique is employed in conjunction with hypnosis through external control.

I do not know of any case in which a subject in a state of autohypnosis successfully psychoanalyzed himself, although in theory that is not of necessity impossible. Conceivably a subject having a thorough knowledge of the psychoanalytic technique might find that autohypnosis is the proper key to opening the door of memory to the crucial incident. It would be an interesting experiment, if a subject with the requisite background undertook it.

A simple method of teaching autohypnosis is to make the posthypnotic suggestion that when the subject thereafter counts to five, he will fall into an hypnotic sleep, but will retain sufficient consciousness to make mental suggestions to his own subjective mind which will have continuing effect, and also to awaken himself when he desires to do so by counting to ten.

In teaching autohypnosis to a subject, it is unnecessary to train him in all its facets. Time in training and risk of misuse are both reduced by confining the instruction to what is essential for the desired therapeutic purpose. A subject learning autohypnosis as a means of overcoming insomnia, for instance, need not, and in most cases should not, be concerned with regression, anaesthesia and many other hypnotic effects; yet knowledge of autohypnosis, to counter insomnia alone, is a valuable asset to the person so afflicted.

With regard to posthypnotic suggestion through autohypnosis, a word of caution should be given. Once the autohypnotic technique is mastered by the subject, he may utilize it, not only to give himself the posthypnotic suggestions originally contemplated, but also any others which he may subsequently fancy. Therein lies a danger. He may, for example, employ his knowledge to create an anaesthesia to relieve pain which is actually organic in origin, and thus neglect nature's warnings with unfortunate effects. Autohypnosis should therefore be taught only to subjects with sufficient intelligence to use it wisely and within limits. They should be warned against its misuse, and admonished never to use it in any situation unless a physician has determined that the difficulty complained of is nonorganic.

CHAPTER FIVE

Therapeutic Application
(AUTOSUGGESTION AND SUBJECTIVELY CONTROLLED
SLUMBER)

THE SUBJECT of autosuggestion in the waking state, as distinguished from autohypnosis, is, strictly speaking, not a part of the subject matter of this treatise. It is sufficiently allied to it, however, by virtue of the fact that its phenomena are explained by the same underlying theory, so that a few words concerning it are appropriate here.

Autosuggestion involves the conscious process of repeating mentally a thought or phrase representing the desired physical reaction or mental attitude: "Every day in every way I'm feeling better and better." This process results in the establishment of a similar thought pattern which manifests itself in the desired physical reaction or mental attitude, if organically feasible.

The conscious autosuggestion may achieve its result by affecting the objective mind directly. This is obviously quite different from the process of autohypnosis in which the objective consciously controls (and suggests to) the subjective which it has allowed to come to the fore.

There is an intermediate process between these two, which embodies simplicity of method with positive practical results; I refer to the influencing of one's own subjective in ordinary sleep (without autohypnosis) through conscious mental repetition of the desired thought pattern while one is in the process of going into the state of ordinary slumber. Because it results in control of the subjective thought pattern (but not in the manner resulting from external hypnosis or autohypnosis), I call it subjectively controlled slumber.

As the relaxation and recession of the objective senses proceed towards the point where sleep occurs, the subjective is concomitantly coming to the fore. During this time one may consciously repeat mentally the thought or phrase representing the desired physical reaction or mental attitude; and this repetition influences the subjective which is in the process of coming to the fore, and implants itself as the basic, controlling accepted generalization of the subjective, and thus remains with it in this capacity during the ensuing period of sleep (until otherwise dispelled).

In this way one is able to establish for himself the basic thought pattern which controls his mental and physical processes, attitudes, and reactions during the sleeping hours, generally with carry-over into the subsequent waking state (for the once established thought pattern will persist until otherwise dispelled).

An understanding of this technique, especially when associated with an appreciation of its theoretical basis, will enable the average person to help himself in this simple but effective way in connection with many of the common disturbances which beset mankind.

Disturbing thoughts may be rejected, attitudes revamped, desires controlled, fears dispelled, hopes nourished; practically everything which is possible through posthypnotic suggestion may be attained to some degree through subjectively controlled slumber.

The conscious mental repetition of the thought or phrase representing the desired physical reaction or mental attitude need not be expressed in precise language; literary quality and exactitude of diction *per se* serve no purpose here. It is only required that the thought or phrase employed have the desired significance to the user.

Actually the same words may be used on different

occasions, each time with variant connotation. One may develop a phrase with inclusive possibilities and employ it under divers conditions. It is an individual matter in which the significance of the thought or phrase *to the user* is the only criterion of its value.

For myself, I often employ the sentence: "I'll sleep soundly, and wake up well." It has comprehensive significance, and is conducive to almost instantaneous sleep as well as postslumber euphoria. I find that deep breathing is also apt to induce sleep quickly, and generally adjust the first phrase to a deeply taken and moderately held inhalation and the second phrase to a relaxed exhalation. The combination of this breathing and thought pattern results in a smooth release to sleep. The thought pattern itself not only serves as a formula for subjectively controlled slumber with carry-over into the waking state, but also aids in the achievement of the relaxation and objective recession which are requisite for sleep.

Incidentally, the problem of torpid wakefulness following interrupted nocturnal slumber may be attacked through an understanding of what causes such restlessness. It is often accompanied by the involuntary repetition of some thought pattern which has taken control of the subjective mind. Paradoxical as it seems, the best way to attack the problem is consciously to awaken one's self, and to reject and dispel the repetitious thought pattern, and then to

recommence the relaxation process towards sleep,
employing one's ordinary pattern of relaxation or
that of subjectively controlled slumber. The conscious reawakening brings the objective to the fore,
thus making possible the active rejection of the troublesome thought pattern; this rejection is accomplished by arriving at a generalization of rejection,
which requires an inductive process, of which the
objective alone is capable. That is why the reawakening (bringing the objective to the fore) must precede the return to sleep.

CHAPTER SIX

Other Theories

THE SCIENTIFIC FORMULA-
tion of the etiology of psychic phenomena is still in
the dynamic stage.

The literature of hypnosis abounds with attempted
explanations of that phenomenon alone. Braid, who
adhered to the theory of monoideism and ideomotor
action, maintained that hypnotic phenomena resulted solely from the fact that ideas reacted on the
body and produced their physical equivalent. Salter
claims hypnosis is "nothing but an aspect of conditioning." Janet and Prince conceived a dissociation
theory based upon a concept of double consciousness, that is two consciousnesses simultaneously co-
existing, but they made no attempt to distinguish

between them. Hull contends that hypnosis is merely a state of relatively heightened susceptibility to prestige suggestion.

I find none of these theories satisfying. The terms "monoideism" and "ideomotor action" serve as labels which describe the effects, but they fail to supply any concept of cause. The similarity between hypnotic phenomena and various results of conditioning does not prove that hypnotism and conditioning are identical. Though the horse and the zebra are similar, they are yet distinct from each other. Some subjects are hypnotizable even at their first session in a matter of seconds, in less time than it takes to condition them. The dissociation theory got onto the right track but stopped at the wrong station. It did not go on to explain the difference between the two consciousnesses (my "two minds"), nor how and within what limits they act upon and react towards each other. This defect was fatal, and it underlies the conclusion of Hull (cf. C. L. Hull, *Hypnosis and Suggestibility*, Appleton-Century, 1933) that the results of Messerschmidt and Mitchell "suggest rather strongly that the whole concept of dissociation as functional independence is an error." If the results of these investigators had been evaluated in the light of the seesaw balance factor of my Theory of Psychic Relative Exclusion, the conclusion would have been different. For example, Hull summarizes Messerschmidt's results: "The simultaneous execution of tasks in the dissociated condition enormously reduces the score from that which is obtained by the conscious performance of but a single task," and he concludes that this indicates that the dissociation concept is erroneous. But the seesaw balance factor of my theory accounts for the variability in the performances. Where one of the tasks is performed by the objective and the other by the subjective, neither mind is as fully to the fore as it would be if the other were dormant. Of the two, the recessive (Messerschmidt's subconscious) performs less efficiently than its dominant counterpart (Messerschmidt's conscious), while the dominant mind is still somewhat impeded to the extent to which the recessive is at all active; and thus even the dominant mind functions less efficiently than it would if it alone were acting. Thus the seesaw balance factor of the Theory of Psychic Relative Exclusion explains the variability in the performances, and Messerschmidt's experimental findings, which destroy the old dissociation concept, serve to confirm the theory herein propounded. Hull's conclusion that hypnosis is merely a state of relatively heightened susceptibility to prestige suggestion fails in any event to explain the fact that persons may be hypnotized by phonograph records alone, as was described by G. H. Estabrooks in 1930 in "A Standardized Hypnotic Technique Dictated to a Victrola Record" which appeared in the *American Journal of Psychology*.

Hull's conclusion that "hypnosis is not sleep, that it has no special relationship to sleep, and that the whole concept of sleep when applied to hypnosis obscures rather than clarifies the situation" is also erroneous. Hull bases that statement upon the results of experiments which demonstrated that differences exist between certain physical responses in the sleeping and the hypnotic states. Those experiments had established: (1) That in the trance state the patellar reflex resembled the reaction in the waking state more closely than it did in natural sleep, (2) That voluntary responses to stimuli in the waking and the trance states were similar, while in natural sleep they were retarded almost to obliteration, and (3) That conditioned reflexes may be set up during hypnosis as they can in the waking state, and cannot during natural sleep. All of these differences between hypnotic and natural sleep, in which the physical responses during hypnotic trance are more like those of a person awake than like those of a person asleep, are predictable from, and in terms of, the Theory of Psychic Relative Exclusion. They follow from the fact that "hypnotic sleep differs from ordinary sleep in that it is induced by the hypnotist," and that in the course of such induction, the hypnotist brings the subjective mind of the subject to the fore. "But instead of coming to the fore as in ordinary sleep, without being controlled by, or subject to, any other mind, it comes to the fore with the expectation of being controlled by, and subject to, the suggestions of the hypnotist. This expectation of the subjective mind is in the nature of an accepted generalization, and this explains the hypnotist's resultant control" (cf. Chapter 2 *supra*). This explains those experimental results upon which Hull relied. In the hypnotic state of the subjects in those experiments their subjective minds had come to the fore with the expectation of being controlled by the stimuli (suggestions) which might be directed to them, e.g. (1) by the patellar thump, (2) by the stimuli for voluntary responses, and (3) by the suggestions which produced the conditioned reflexes.

Thus the Theory of Psychic Relative Exclusion, while it is founded upon a fundamental similarity in structure between hypnotic and ordinary sleep (the subjective-objective shift), at the same time explains the differences between the physical responses observed in those experiments. Hull erred in making the assumption that the differences between the physical manifestations of hypnotic and ordinary sleep resulted from a difference in their fundamental natures—an assumption without logical or pragmatic foundation.

Freud, incidentally, refers to the kinship between sleep and hypnosis in his *Group Psychology and the Analysis of the Ego,* saying:

"The command to sleep in hypnosis means nothing more or less than an order to withdraw all interest from the world and to concentrate it upon the person of the hypnotist. And it is so understood by the subject; for in this withdrawal of interest from the outer world lies the psychological characteristic of sleep and the kinship between sleep and the state of hypnosis is based upon it."

Attempts have been made to explain what hypnosis is in terms of psychoanalytic terminology. The so-called psychoanalytic theory describes it as the result of the subject's desire to be controlled by a person who resembles a parent, or as the result of the subject's desire for gratification of unconscious erotic or masochistic drives. The motivational theory defines it in terms of purposeful striving to behave like a hypnotized person as described by the hypnotist. It has further been suggested that in hypnotism the hypnotist becomes the subject's super-ego; and also that submission to hypnosis represents the gratification of a latent desire for protection or security. It appears to me that although some of these factors may be present in some instances, they will be absent in others. Both the conscious and subconscious (objective and subjective) factors which impel a subject to submit to hypnosis differ from subject to subject, depending upon the interplay of all the reactions to the diversified experiences of his life which help differentiate each individual from every other; and by the same token every subject reacts to a particular hypnotist in a unique manner, different from that of the same subject to any other hypnotist, and different from that of all other subjects to the same hypnotist. Thus these psychoanalytic concepts are helpful towards an understanding of the differences in the reactions of various subjects; but for this very reason they fail to supply any comprehensive interpretation of the phenomena common to *all* hypnoses.

Just this—a comprehensive interpretation of the phenomena common to *all* hypnoses—is what the Theory of Psychic Relative Exclusion attempts to supply. I believe it explains them as herein described. The theory appeals to me further because it also clarifies all the variations of hypnotic phenomena, and it serves at the same time as an exposition of the nature of and the differences between waking and sleeping mental processes, of the nature of and differences between daydreams and nightdreams, of the nature of and differences between heterosuggestion and autosuggestion. Finally I advance it because it explains the "why" of Freud's "how": Freud and his followers have principally set forth *how* his psychoanalytic technique works. The Theory of Psychic Relative Exclusion explains *why* it works.

Still it is only a theory, a working hypothesis. I propound it and recommend it in the interest of a scientific understanding of the functioning of the mind in its normal and abnormal states. Its formula-

tion and elucidation here may serve as the means to
a clearer grasp of the true nature of the factors in
the complex domain of thought.

The application of hypnosis to psychotherapy, as
here described, is not new, except perhaps in manner and degree. Spiritual healers even in Biblical
days used it unwittingly. Mesmer, Braid, Liebeault,
Bernheim, Bramwell, Charcot, and others, and even
Freud and Breuer, applied it, each in his own way
and in accordance with his individual concept of the
phenomenon. I believe, however, that none of these
possessed a comprehension of its true nature. Their
use of hypnotism, coming in the early years of its
recognition as a distinct therapeutic instrument, was
of necessity empirical. We are indebted to the records of their endeavors, of their partly developed
methods, of their misgivings, of their failures and
successes, which have furnished us with the groundwork whereon to construct what appears to be a
more solid modern framework of theoretical and
practical exposition of the nature and possibilities of
hypnosis. Applied with the aid of this clearer understanding, it should yield more fruitful results.

Powerful as it is, however, it is not a panacea. The
exact extent to which it may beneficially supplement,
or in specific instances supplant, psychoanalysis
and other forms of psychotherapy, is still subject to
much experimentation, investigation, and scientific
observation before its ultimate boundaries will be

fixed. But this at least I venture to suggest: that its potentialities are vast, and that the Theory of Psychic Relative Exclusion, whether ultimately accepted, modified or rejected in favor of one more satisfying, will prove helpful towards increasingly successful psychotherapy through hypnotic control.

CHAPTER SEVEN

Summary

THE theory of Psychic Relative Exclusion, here developed and applied, is advanced by the author as a working hypothesis for psychotherapy through hypnotic control.

It explains the manifestations of the mind when awake, or asleep, or hypnotized. It accounts for the difference between our thought processes when awake and when asleep; for the absurdity of some dreams and the wish-fulfillment nature of others; for the effectiveness of the methods by which external hypnotic control is obtained, extended, and relinquished; for the increased memory ability of a hypnotized subject, and for the potency of posthypnotic suggestions; for the ability of a subject to hypnotize himself, or to reorganize his mental processes through autosuggestion or through subjectively controlled slumber. It explains why the Freudian psychoanalytic technique works and also how psychotherapy through hypnotic control (hypnoanalysis) achieves the desired results. It furnishes a basis for the effectual application of the methods and techniques here described, and serves as a foundation for their scientific extension to variant types of psychotherapeutic investigation.

How vast the scope of this branch of healing is we can appreciate when we consider that our contemporary civilization, which both scales the heights and plumbs the depths the mind and soul of man can reach, subjects all to such multifarious pressures and conflicts, often of traumatic force, that psychic disturbances and neurotic disorders are becoming increasingly common. To cope with these problems, the author anticipates that hypnoanalysis and posthypnotic suggestion for psychotherapy will in time widely supplement, though they may not supersede, the technique of waking free association or the use of suggestion alone, because of the greater speed and efficacy attainable through hypnotic control.

PART TWO

Hypnosis—
Technique and Specific Application

CHAPTER EIGHT

Securing Hypnotic Control

THE GREAT MAJORITY of normally intelligent persons between the ages of 15 and 55 can be hypnotized; and of those below and above that age group there is evidence that many, if not most, between 5 and 15, and over 55, can also be hypnotically controlled.

External hypnotic control of the subject is achieved by the hypnotist in one way: he induces the objective mind of the subject to recede, thus bringing the subjective mind of the subject to the fore with the expectation of being controlled by, and subject to, the suggestions of the hypnotist.

There are numerous ways in which this may be accomplished. The choice of method depends upon the ease with which the hypnotist is able to influence the particular subject. This may be determined upon the basis of certain preliminary tests and from the reactions of the subject while being hypnotized. Fundamentally all the methods are similar in that they are an attempt to induce the subject to think of something so insignificant that for all practical purposes the subject is thinking of nothing at all. In this way the subject's senses are reduced to a passive state, his objective mind consequently receding, and the subjective concomitantly coming to the fore with the expectation of hypnotic influence already implanted as the result of prior conversation.

Physical and mental relaxation on the part of the subject is essential before hypnotic control can be established. The following are some simple tests to determine whether that condition exists:

A. *Falling Backward.* Have the subject stand, feet together, back to you, facing a wall or corner of a room, concentrating on some point above, which forces the sight direction about 45 degrees upward. Suggest that the subject relax and listen only to you. Emphasize relaxation of the whole body. Suddenly give the subject a slight pull backward: he should fall back easily. If he does, you may proceed. If not, he has not been sufficiently relaxed; explain that to him and try again.

Point out that he must relax, as that is the first step towards hypnosis; that he must cooperate with you; that it is not a question of your mind being stronger than his, but rather of mutual cooperation which produces the result. Assure him against fear of falling backward; state that you will brace his fall. If difficulty is encountered, try pushing your palm against the subject's shoulder blades, and then quickly releasing the pressure. This often results in his falling back easily.

Repeated explanations and trials will generally lead to positive results with the great majority of subjects. This test has several advantages. It enables you to determine when relaxation has been achieved; it provides a basis for teaching the subject how to relax; and the success you achieve is conducive to further cooperation of the subject.

When the subject is relaxed, have him assume the original position again, and then say, "Think only of one thought—the thought that you are falling backwards." If the subject is relaxed, a positive response will follow. Brace the fall for him.

Sometimes it is necessary to add in a steady, monotonous voice: ". . . That you're falling backwards. Just think of falling backwards now—backwards—backwards——. Don't resist——. Here you come."

Sometimes at the point of falling backwards the subject's objective mind has sufficiently receded so that the suggestion "Sleep" is sufficient to establish control. This is unusual, but occasionally occurs. An experienced hypnotist can judge the probability of success by the degree of abandon in the fall.

B. *Falling Forward.* Have the subject stand, as for the falling-backward response, except facing you. Say, "Now think of only one thought—that you are falling forward," etc. as for the falling-backward response. The falling-forward is the more difficult response to achieve, and should generally be attempted only after the falling-backward response has been successful.

In some cases women who wear high heels, however, will resist the falling-backward response, but will obey the falling-forward.

A & B: *Eyes Closed.* Both the falling-backward and the falling-forward responses may be induced with increased rapidity if the subject is directed to close his eyes. The fact that the eyes are closed gives greater scope to the force of your suggestions alone, and prevents counter-impulses which sometimes occur when a recalcitrant subject observes his own movements.

C. *Arm Stiffening.* Have the subject stand, facing you, about eight feet distant. Tell him to raise his right arm, palm up. Order him to look at your eyes, and arrest his attention with your gaze. Continue: "Stretch it out as far as you can. Now I'm going to make it stiff. Extend it as far as you can, as rigid and straight as you possibly can." Wait about fifteen seconds. "You can stretch it further. As far as you can now. Straight and rigid. It's stiff, straight and rigid now. Keep your eyes on mine and you can't bend it. *You can't bend it now.* Try and you'll see that you can't. You can't do it." Keep the subject's eyes fixed with your gaze, and in the great majority of cases he will not be able to bend his arm.

Let him try for about ten seconds, or half a minute if your control appears good. Before he succeeds in bending it himself, say: "Now when I count to three, you can bend it. 1—2—3. Relax. You can bend it now." Avert your eyes at the same time.

D. *Chevraul's Pendulum.* The pendulum consists of a small metal weight attached to a string about thirty inches long. It is held by the subject by means of a small ring attached to the upper end of the string. The ring is passed onto the subject's index finger. Place a plain (unmagnetized) metal bar on the floor or table under the metal weight.

Tell the subject that the metal bar is magnetized and that its properties are such that the weight will swing in the direction of the bar. In the hands of a suggestible subject, the weight will begin to swing after a few moments, in the suggested direction. Change the direction of the bar, and within a few seconds the direction of the swing will change correspondingly. Place a "magnetized" circle under it, and the weight will swing in a circle. Remove the bar and the circle, and the weight will come to a stop.

You may then explain to the subject that in fact

the bar and the circle were not at all magnetized, and that actually the weight reacted as it did only because the subject unconsciously moved it as the result of your controlling his subconscious (subjective) mind.

Once the foregoing responses, or some of them, have been established, a large variety of procedures may be used to induce hypnotic sleep. Some of these may be outlined as follows:

1. *Voice Alone.* In securing hypnotic control by ʁse of the voice alone the hypnotist utilizes his voice for a number of coordinated purposes. The tone quality must be soothing to the subject at the same time that the manner of delivery arrests and holds his attention. The words must be carefully chosen to serve as effective motivation for cooperative recession of the objective interests. The language suggested in the following paragraph is not unalterable, but rather variable within the limits outlined in the note appended to it.

Have the subject lie on a couch or sit comfortably in a chair. Suggest that he think only of what you say, and listen only to your voice.

Intone: "Just think of sleep now, that you are getting tired and want to go to sleep. That you're very tired, your eyes are getting heavy, your body is limp, your head is heavy. That you're very sleepy and you want to go to sleep. Just think of sleep now, that you're very tired and want to go to sleep. That your

body is limp and heavy, your head is heavy. You're
so tired; your eyelids are getting heavier and heavier,
and you want to close your heavy eyelids and go to
sleep. That you want to close your heavy eyelids and
go to sleep. That you're relaxed and comfortable,
that you're breathing deeply, that you're perfectly
comfortable and so tired. That you want to go to
sleep. That you're going to close your heavy eyelids
and go to sleep. That you're going to close your
heavy eyelids now and go to sleep. Just think of
sleep now, that you're going to close your heavy eyelids and go to sleep."

And as they begin to close, or flutter: "That your
eyes are closing. You're very comfortable, and very
tired and want to go to sleep. That you're so tired,
that your eyes are so tired, that you can't keep them
open any longer, and you're going to close your eyes
and go to sleep. That you want to go to sleep. That
your eyes are closing now." Sometimes the direct
suggestion, "Close your eyes now," is necessary.

"That your eyes are closed now. That you're very
tired and that you're going into a deep sleep. That
you're so tired, that you want to go into a deep sleep.
That you're going into a deep sleep. That you're
passing into a state of deep, comfortable sleep. That
you're going into a deep sleep now and you're going
to stay fast asleep until I tell you to wake up. I'm
going to count to twenty now and as I do, you're
going into a very deep sleep and when I get to

twenty, you'll take a deep breath, relax all over and be in a deep comfortable sleep and you'll stay asleep until I tell you to wake up." Count to twenty in a slow, monotonous voice. Wait for a deep breath. If necessary add: "Take a deep breath now."

Then: "That you're fast asleep now; you're comfortable; you're breathing deeply." (Pause. Subject will breathe deeply.) "You hear only my voice, listen only to me, do only as I say. You'll stay fast asleep until I tell you to wake up."

Note: The language above may be varied, expanded or reduced as occasion requires; but the same thought pattern should be developed and maintained. Observe the continuity of the pattern in relation to the desired effects.

"Just think of sleep now"—concentration on one thought. "That you—want to go to sleep"—imperceptible emphasis that it is the subject's wish. ". . . Your eyes are getting heavy . . . you're very sleepy"—gradual development followed by repetition of ". . . you *want* to go to sleep. . . ." Then comes further development in the suggestion that the eyelids *begin* to get heavy, leading to ". . . you want to close your *heavy eyelids* and go to sleep." Then: "That you're going to close your heavy eyelids *now* . . ." followed by "that your eyes *are closing* . . ." and ". . . you're going to close your eyes and *go to sleep*," and so forth.

Reread the suggested monologue, and analyze the

unfolding of the ideas. Note the gradual development, timed repetition, adumbration of subsequent
steps, commencing with emphasis on the subject's
own thought (". . . *you* want to go to sleep . . ."),
followed by the direct statements from the hypnotist
"That your eyes are closed now . . . that you'll stay
fast asleep until I tell you to wake up."

Do not memorize the words, but do master the
development of the thought pattern.

The lighting and surroundings should be unob-
trusive: the source of light preferably in back of the
subject, diffused, not too bright; the furnishings,
pictures, etc. not in the subject's line of vision. The
voice should be medium low, slow and soothing, yet
firm and unhesitant. Talk with quiet conviction. Do
not domineer.

The hypnotist may stand (or sit) in front of, be-
side or behind the subject. It is best to be in a
position to observe the subject's eyes, as they are a
ready gauge of the progress toward sleep and thus
advise the hypnotist when to accelerate or retard his
activity.

2. *Sight Fixation.* Similar monologue may be employed in conjunction with visual fixation of the subject's attention. The point of concentration may be a
pencil point on a blank wall, or a source of light
(pencil-type flashlight or candlelight), or a small
shiny object (diamond or rhinestone against a black
background or attached to the end of a black stick or

pencil), or a dentist's mirror reflecting light emanating from behind the subject, or a small clear crystal ball.

For example, when using a pencil-type flashlight, have the outer covering black, dark grey or some other light-absorbing color, the bulb or light source small, the light strong enough to demand the focusing of attention but not so bright that it will hurt the subject's eyes. Tell the subject to look only at the light, and to listen only to your voice and think only of what you say. Then add, casually, that if he does so, he'll soon be asleep. Have him relax in a comfortable chair and look at the light. Hold it about two or three feet in front and one foot above the subject's eye level. Then proceed as in 1 above.

The methods employing other sight fixation points are similar.

3. *Eyes-Counting*. After the subject has relaxed in a comfortable chair, tell him to follow your directions, listen only to your voice, and think of nothing else. Then proceed as follows:

Stand in front of the subject. Direct him to look at a designated spot on your coat, e.g. a button in the direct line of his vision. Tell him you will count; that on 1 he should close his eyes, on 2 open them, on 3 close them, etc. Add that he should follow the count carefully and that soon he'll be fast asleep.

Count fairly rapidly, from one to about twelve;

then continue, gradually lengthening the intervals during which the eyes remain shut.

You will notice that the subject's eyes open less widely as you proceed. Adjust the counting to encourage this diminution.

When the lids merely flutter instead of opening to the count, increase the period of closure further until the flutter becomes almost imperceptible. At this point stop counting for about seven to ten seconds, and then say, in a conversational tone: "You are going into a deep sleep now, a comfortable sleep. I'm going to count to ten now, and when I get to ten, you'll take a deep breath, relax all over, and be in a deep comfortable sleep, and you'll stay fast asleep until I tell you to wake up."

At the beginning of the counting, use a conversational tone. As your pace slackens, however, gradually lower your voice so that you are whispering when the lids flutter. Then, before actually stopping the original count, rapidly grade back to conversational volume. After the seven to ten second pause, continue in, and maintain the conversational tone.

Usually the subject will succumb before you reach 100; however if he does not, then continue counting in the same voice, but starting at one again.

4. *Graduated Control.* Have the subject seated in a comfortable chair. Instruct the subject (1) to remove all rings from his fingers, (2) to relax, (3) to clasp his hands together (intertwining the fingers) in his

lap, (4) to put his feet flat (uncrossed) on the floor, straight down (not thrust forward). Tell him to listen only to you and to concentrate only on what you say, and then continue substantially as follows, in a conversational tone:

"Look down at the point where your thumbs cross, and concentrate on that point." Wait about ten or fifteen seconds. Then slowly and deliberately:

"Relax. Now close your eyes and roll your eyeballs up. Keep your eyes closed and your eyeballs rolled up. As I count to ten, your lids will become tighter and tighter shut, and when I reach 10 you won't be able to open them. 1—2—3—tighter—4—5—lids closer together—6—at 10 they'll be stuck together—7—tighter—closer—tighter together—keep your eyeballs up—8—very tight now—9—10—keep your eyeballs up and you cannot open your eyes. You can try, but you won't be able to."

If the subject is able to open his eyes, explain that he apparently failed to cooperate: he did not keep his eyeballs rolled up, as instructed, or he failed to concentrate on your instructions only. Emphasize that he must dispel all other thoughts and that he can do so if he tries. Point out that it is easier to hypnotize intelligent people because they can best cooperate. Insist that he will surely be hypnotized if he faithfully follows all the given directions. Then start again.

Do not be disheartened by failure, and above all,

do not reveal any discouragement you may feel. Maintain a deliberate manner and conversational tone.

Often a failure in the first attempt is followed by success in the second. Sometimes a few attempts must be made before the eyelids remain shut. Between each attempt, lay the blame squarely upon the subject's failure to follow all the instructions, and impress upon him that success is certain if he co-operates fully.

When the subject makes a reasonable attempt to open his eyes and fails, permit him to try for a few seconds (long enough to be convinced that he cannot open them, but not so long that the spell is broken) and then say:

"Stop trying. Keep your eyes shut. I'm now going to clasp your hands together so that you cannot separate them. As I count from one to ten, your hands will become more and more tightly clasped together and at ten you will not be able to take them apart. Clasp your hands tightly. 1—tighter—2—closer—3—4 (give subject's arms one or two light downward strokes with your finger tips)—your arms are getting numb—5—tighter—closer—6—7—very tight now—tight as you can—8—very tight—fingers are stiff—9—10—they're stuck together. You cannot separate them no matter how hard you try. Try, and you'll see you can't."

Generally they cannot. If they do, you can sometimes succeed by starting this method again, but it may be better to switch to another method (e.g. 2 or 3 above) instead.

When the hands remain clasped, despite the subject's efforts to open them, wait a few moments; then say:

"Stop trying. Stay as you are. Now I'll make your legs stiff so that you won't be able to stand up. As I count to ten, your legs will get stiffer and stiffer, and at ten you won't be able to stand up. 1—2—stiffer— (give the subject's thighs, knees and legs one or two light downward strokes with your fingertips)—3— they're getting numb—4—more numb—5—6—numb and stiff, and you can't feel them—7—stiffer—8—very stiff now—9—10—you can't stand up. You can try, but you won't be able to." As they try: "The harder you try, the harder it is," or "You can move your body, but you can't move your legs."

After a few moments, but longer than for the eyes and hands, say, "All right. Stop trying. (Short pause.) I'm going to put you to sleep now. Relax. Think of sleep now—that you're going to sleep. You're getting tired . . ." etc., continuing with monologue similar to method 1 above, appropriately modified and condensed. Once the eyes are closed, and the hands and feet immobilized, sleep can be induced fairly rapidly.

5. *Mass Hypnosis.* The method outlined in 4 is readily applicable to a large number of subjects at

the same time, and may be used to secure simultaneous control of two or more subjects.

The first three methods above described may also be applied to more than one subject at a time; however, there is a difficulty arising from the fact that the degree to which control is established may differ among the subjects involved. Through its system of graduated control, method 4 overcomes this disadvantage. As each step in the series of controls is achieved, the subjects already influenced to that degree may be maintained at that level, while the others are brought up to a similar point.

Using this method, the author has immobilized all but two or three in a group of about thirty, and then put approximately half of them to sleep simultaneously.

In this connection, consider also method 8 following.

6. *Rapid Control.* The following technique is suggested only to persons who have first successfully conducted a considerable number of hypnoses by some of the slower methods.

Instruct the subject to stand facing you, to remove his rings, to clasp the hands together with fingers intertwined, and to hold them up with arms either parallel to the floor, or elbows bent. Place yourself in front of the subject so that his eyes are on a level with or lower than yours. (If you are shorter in stature than the subject is, have the subject seated

and seat yourself on a slightly higher chair or stool.)
Proceed as follows:

"Keep your eyes fixed on mine. Clasp your hands
together as tightly as you can. Tighter. You can do it
tighter than that. As tightly as you can now. Tighter.
Closer. Tighter. So tight now that you cannot take
them apart. Now you cannot take them apart no
matter how hard you try. —Sleep!"

While you speak, keep the subject's eyes fixed by
the stare of your own. Open your eyes more widely
as you proceed. Speak clearly, directly, imperatively
(but do not shout), with clipped rapidity. As you
speak, press the subject's hands together with the
palms of your hands cupped over his clasped ones.
As soon as you believe he is squeezing his hands
together *as tightly as he can,* remove your hands and
utter the last sentence, but not yet the word "Sleep."
Keep the subject's eyes fixed with your stare. When
he tries, and fails to take his hands apart for two or
three seconds, pass your right palm over his eyes and
quickly command: "Sleep!"

If his eyes do not close, add: "Close your eyes and
go to sleep." And then: "Deeper to sleep," etc. for a
few seconds.

With this method, the experienced hypnotist can
gain control of his subject in a matter of seconds.

7. *Second Sleep.* Having first hypnotized a subject
by one of the slower methods, the hypnotist may
give a posthypnotic suggestion that the subject, after

being awakened, will go to sleep a second time upon a given signal, e.g. upon the count of 10 by the hypnotist. Before counting to ten to induce this second sleep, the hypnotist should have the subject seated comfortably, and then direct him to look at the hypnotist's raised index finger held before the subject's eyes. The count to ten follows at the rate of about one second per number, in a direct, arresting manner, conversational tone modulating to softer as the count proceeds.

At the count of ten, if the subject's eyes have already closed, merely add: "Sleep! You're fast asleep now." If the eyes are still open at the count of ten, add: "Close your eyes and go to sleep . . ." etc.

8. *Sleep following Light Trance.* This is similar to method 7 except that the subject is merely put into a very light trance in the first instance.

Have the subject seated and relaxed; proceed as in method 4, through eyelid catalepsy only. (Some prefer to include the hand clasp response as well.) Then say: "I'm going to awaken you in a moment and will then put you to sleep again—into a deep sleep. When I count to ten, you'll relax, close your eyes and go into a very deep sleep. Soon after I awaken you now, I'll count to ten, and you'll relax, close your eyes and go into a deep, comfortable sleep. Now when I snap my fingers, you'll wake up." Wait a moment; then snap your fingers, saying, "Wake up—open your eyes."

Then, having allowed only a short time to elapse, approach the subject, who is still seated. Wear a simple ring with a centralized stone on your right hand, and hold the back of your hand over his eye level and slightly to the front so that he must look up to see it. *Very quickly and in a soft, low voice:* "Look at the ring. 1, 2, 3, 4, 5, 6, 7, 8, 9, 10. Close your eyes and go to sleep." (Quickly turn your hand and bring the palm down over the subject's forehead and eyes.) "Sleep, sleep, sleep, sleep, sleep, sleep; you're going into a deep sleep, fast asleep, fast asleep. You're fast asleep, fast asleep; you're fast asleep; you're fast asleep." Then slower: "You're fast asleep, in a deep comfortable sleep. You hear only my voice and you're going to stay fast asleep until I tell you to wake up."

Of the two parts of this process, light trance and deep sleep, the former may take between five and ten minutes, but the latter requires less than sixty seconds. The directions for the latter should be given *quickly* and in a soft, low voice. The intervening period should be kept to a minimum especially with subjects who have never been hypnotized before, though even a five minute interval is not necessarily too long.

This method may thus be used to hypnotize a number of persons at once. The first part of the process is applied to a large group simultaneously. Those who do not respond are eliminated. The others, having been first "awakened" *en masse*, are then quickly put to sleep one at a time, as here described. During the second part of the process, speaking quickly, and going from one to another rapidly, you may secure control over five or six persons in about two to three minutes.

While teaching persons to hypnotize, I have observed that beginners often mix their methods; they employ part of one in conjunction with part of another. This generally results in failure. Only one method at a time should be attempted. If it fails, abandon it completely before undertaking a new one.

Although the language of securing control refers to "deep sleep," actually a quick deep sleep is obtained only in rare instances. In most cases, the original control is of a slight degree, and must be maintained and extended carefully by the methods described in the following chapter.

During the process of securing control, an undisturbed atmosphere is essential. Other persons present should refrain from talk, laughter, movement, or any activity which may deter the subject from paying concentrated attention solely to the hypnotist.

The foregoing are the principal methods of securing hypnotic control. The hypnotist may develop his individual variations based upon his own experience. Of course, success may be achieved by *modus operandi* alone; but I have found that adherence to the fundamental theory here outlined has been conducive to intelligent and fruitful development of method towards ease and rapidity in securing, maintaining, and extending control.

If attempts to hypnotize by one method fail, explain to the subject that perhaps another method will be more suitable to him, and change to another method without indicating any embarrassment or frustration you may inwardly feel, for the revelation of any such attitude on your part will act as a suggestion to the subject that you anticipate failure and thus nullify your further efforts. Actually, there is no reason for discomfiture on your part, merely because one method fails. Very often the shift to a different method results in fairly rapid success, even though previous attempts were unavailing. It is advantageous to remind the subject that you cannot hypnotize him against his will, that his active cooperation is essential, and that if he has a strong mind, he can control his mental processes and force himself to cooperate with you.

CHAPTER NINE

Maintaining and Extending Hypnotic Control

W HEN you believe the subject is asleep, proceed as follows:

1. Direct him to unclasp his hands at the count of five and place them, one on each knee (or if he is standing, loosely at his sides). Then say:

"Hold your right hand out, palm up." Place a coin on the palm. "Now as I count to twenty, the coin will get heavier with each number counted, and as I approach twenty, it will become so very heavy that it will weigh your hand down; your hand will droop towards the floor until the coin drops off." Count slowly; at ten add: "It's getting so heavy now you cannot keep it up, and when I reach twenty, the weight will force your hand down until the coin drops off." Continue to twenty. If the hand has not begun to drop, add: "It's beginning to fall downward; down, down, down . . ." etc. until the hand droops towards the floor and the coin falls off. "Now it's not heavy any more and you can raise it again. Raise it." When it is horizontal again, say:

"Now I'll make your hand very light. As I count to ten, your right arm and hand will become lighter and lighter, as light as a little feather, and your hand will rise by itself and float in the air." Count slowly.

If it does not rise, add: "It's beginning to rise now —it's rising now—you can't keep it down any longer—" etc. You may suggest that when you blow on it, it will rise. Then blow, or even give it a slight initial upward push.

After it rises considerably, apparently beyond the subject's volitional control, say: "At the count of three it will fall and resume its original position." Count. After the fall add: "Now as I count to five, your right arm and hand will become normal again. They won't be light any more, and they'll be normal again just like the left." Count, more rapidly this time.

Always remember to renormalize by such countersuggestion any function or senses which you have influenced through any original suggestion of an abnormal nature. If this precaution is neglected, the subject may remain inhibited by the original suggestion. Such inhibition might be automatically resolved as the subject's objective mind later comes to the fore (in waking). On the other hand, the very fact of the physical manifestation of the mental inhibition may augment the force of the suggestion and thus endow it with posthypnotic force, with resultant unpleasantness to the subject over a long period of time.

In any case, however, the renormalizing process is merely a matter of simple hypnotic suggestion, and may generally be accomplished with the subject in light trance, and sometimes even in the waking state.

2. Use similar procedure to make the subject's hand so heavy that he cannot raise it no matter how hard he tries: ". . . it will become as heavy as a ton of lead, and you won't be able to move it . . ." (Avoid unusual or "literary" language. The more trite and obvious the simile, the more acceptable it will be to the subjective, which cannot reason inductively.) Then, let him try to raise it, but he will not be able to. (Renormalize it by countersuggestion and have him raise it once again quickly to indicate its normal reaction.)

2A. In the same way the subject's legs may be immobilized: "As I count to ten your legs will get stiffer and stiffer, and when I get to ten you won't be able to move them, you won't be able to stand up." When you reach five or six in the counting, add: "Stiffer, stiffer; at ten you won't be able to move them, you won't be able to stand up." Right after ten, state: "Now they're stiff and rigid. You can't stand up—no matter how hard you try. Try and you'll see you can't." If the subject begins to move, say: "You can wriggle, but you can't stand up—you cannot do it."

2B. This may be followed by induced aphonia. Speak more quickly and with somewhat added assurance of tone: "As I count to five, your throat will become parched, and when I get to five, you won't be able to speak, until I say you can. 1-2-3-4-5. You cannot speak now. Try to—you cannot do it now."

The hypnotist derives a double advantage from securing the suggested responses to the above procedures:

(a) These procedures constitute a test of whether or not the subject is asleep, and the success of the response is a measure of the hypnotist's control. If the response is poor, further suggestion of sleep may be necessary. Suggestion of control *per se* may be added: "Now you hear only my voice. You will pay attention only to what I say, and do only what I tell you to."

(b) A positive response automatically emphasizes the subject's concentration upon the suggestions of the hypnotist, which in turn furthers the recession of the subject's objective mind, and thus accelerates the process which results in stronger control.

As previously indicated, once control has been established, it may be maintained and extended at the will of the hypnotist. The hypnotist may suggest: "Deeper to sleep," or "As I count to ten, you will go into a deeper sleep," or "You are fast asleep and will stay fast asleep until I tell you to wake up," or "You are comfortable, fast asleep, and nothing disturbs you; you can hear my voice; you hear only my voice, listen only to me, and do only as I say," or any combination or variation which the hypnotist prefers.

Often the use of only the sentence last suggested is sufficient. Continuation of suggestions along specific lines follows, and the very fact of continued suggestions (properly graduated in force) is conducive both to maintenance and extension of the control.

Intelligent gradation of the force of suggestions is important. Since suggestibility varies directly with the depth of trance, suggestions should be limited to those which have a definite potential of acceptance. Progression should therefore be so gradual that positive results are always assured.

Remember that although hypnotic control has been achieved (i.e. the subject's subjective mind has been brought to the fore with the expectation of being controlled by the hypnotist), nevertheless the subject's objective mind is not obliterated. Both the objective and the subjective minds are ever present in a state of seesaw balance. The point to which the hypnotic control extends at any particular time depends upon the *degree* to which the subject's objective mind has receded and the subjective has been concomitantly brought to the fore.

To the extent that the subject's objective mind is still active (and it is always active in some degree), there is the possibility of countersuggestion by the subject's objective mind; and the more unusual, abnormal (to the subject), or bizarre the hypnotist's suggestion may be, the greater is the probability of such countersuggestion overcoming or neutralizing the suggestions from the hypnotist.

When the subject is in a light trance, even slightly abnormal suggestions may thus become ineffective: the suggestion, for instance, that a paper flower is a rose and smells like one. This same suggestion, with the subject in a deeper state of hypnosis (i.e. with his objective mind more receded), will readily take effect.

In the same way, the extent to which some beliefs, tenets and principles of the subject may, while some may not, be overcome, depends upon the *degree* to which the control has been established.

Proper gradation of the force of suggestions is important for the same reasons that the hand-lightening and hand-weighting procedures are significant:

(a) The positiveness of the response is a measure of the degree of control achieved up to that point, and

(b) A positive response emphasizes the subject's concentration upon the suggestions of the hypnotist, which in turn furthers the recession of the subject's objective mind and thus accelerates the process which results in stronger control.

Conversely, a negative response (the result of effective countersuggestion by the subject's objective mind) automatically reduces the control because it permits the objective to assume and maintain a positive position, thus bringing it more actively to the fore. Thus each successful countersuggestion by the subject's objective mind reduces the extent of hypnotic control to some degree.

I might interpolate that this accounts for the fact that upon the removal of the hypnotist while the subject is under his control, whether such withdrawal is voluntary or due to sudden death or disability, the subject will pass into a state of natural sleep and then awaken in due course. This follows from the fact that, once the suggestions of the hypnotist cease, the subject's objective mind comes gradually to the fore because of the lack of suggestions from the hypnotist. The subjective, relieved of such suggestions, and not being capable of the inductive process and therefore lacking initiative, becomes less active, and failing to receive suggestions from the hypnotist over a period of time, loses the expectation of being so controlled. Its motivation thereafter derives from the subject's objective mind

alone. The consequent condition, then, is one of natural sleep. Once a state of ordinary sleep is reached,
the waking process follows in normal course.

Failure to graduate the type of suggestion to
correspond with the degree of control may result in
complete loss of control—i.e. a sudden waking of the
subject. For as a negative response automatically reduces the degree of control *because it permits the
objective to assume a role of positive play, thus
bringing it to the fore in greater degree,* so a very
decidedly negative response (the result of a particularly strong countersuggestion by the subject's objective mind) may bring the objective to the fore to
such a great degree that the subjective will be forced
to the background with resulting loss of control
(waking).

If this should happen, it is advisable for the hypnotist to reinduce sleep quickly. This can generally
be accomplished rapidly by ordering the subject to
close his eyes, relax and think only of sleep. He
should be told that he is going to sleep quickly at
the count of ten, and then the hypnotist should
count in a soft conversational tone at about one second intervals. If spectators' murmurs may distract
from the subject's concentration on the hypnotist, he
should raise his voice sufficiently to overcome the
distraction. Even if only a light state of sleep is
achieved, that is sufficient for the purpose, to wit:
that the hypnotist suggest that he will awaken the

subject at the count of five, and that the subject will then awaken feeling well, wide-awake, happy, without headache or after-effects. This will prevent any headache or unpleasantness due to the sudden awakening.

Exactly what constitutes a proper gradation of the force of suggestions, is a matter which varies from case to case, depending upon divers factors, including the external conditions surrounding the operation, the ability of the hypnotist, the suggestibility of the subject, and the personal equation between the particular hypnotist and the particular subject at the time. What may constitute a natural suggestion to one subject and be readily acceptable by him, may be more abnormal to another subject, and therefore demand a deeper degree of hypnotic control. For example, the suggestion that a subject take off his shoes is generally accepted and acted upon by most persons even in a light state of hypnotic sleep; nevertheless some subjects have been encountered who will strongly resist this apparently simple suggestion, and who must be put into a deep state of sleep before they will act upon it.

Before outlining a *modus operandi* conducive to the desired gradation of the force of suggestions, it might be well to say a preliminary word about the degrees of hypnotic control. Davis and Husband have outlined an Hypnotic Susceptibility Scoring System, numerically graded (Davis, L. W., and

Husband, R. W., "A Study of Hypnotic Susceptibility in Relation to Personality Traits," *Journal of Abnormal and Social Psychology*, 26:175-182, 1931). Their pragmatic conclusion is that ". . . it was only very rarely that the more difficult suggestions were successful when the simpler ones had failed." Their chart is as follows:

HYPNOTIC SUSCEPTIBILITY SCORING SYSTEM OF DAVIS & HUSBAND

Depth	Score	Objective Symptoms
Insusceptible	0	
Hypnoidal	1	
	2	Relaxation
	3	Fluttering of lids
	4	Closing of eyes
	5	Complete physical relaxation
Light trance	6	Catalepsy of eyes
	7	Limb catalepsies
	10	Rigid catalepsy
	11	Anaesthesia (glove)
Medium trance	13	Partial amnesia
	15	Posthypnotic anaesthesia
	17	Personality changes
	18	Simple posthypnotic suggestions
	20	Kinaesthetic delusions; complete amnesia

	21	Ability to open eyes without affecting trance
	23	Bizarre posthypnotic suggestions
	25	Complete somnambulism
	26	Positive visual hallucinations, posthypnotic
Somnambulistic trance	27	Positive auditory hallucinations, posthypnotic
	28	Systemized posthypnotic amnesias
	29	Negative auditory hallucinations
	30	Negative visual hallucinations; hyperaesthesias

This scoring system has been accepted by many psychologists as an index of the gradation of suggestibility. Under the theory here expounded, it would constitute an index of the results of the gradation of the force of suggestions made.

In the light of the foregoing we may now consider the extension of control, once the hand-lightening and hand-weighting responses are satisfactory.

3. Establish mutual vocal contact. Say: "Now when I speak to you, you'll be able to hear me and then to answer me, even though you'll remain asleep all the time. You're comfortable, aren't you?"

Wait for the response. At the beginning it is slower than in the waking state. The subject's voice is also softer. If the subject does not answer, or seems to have difficulty in vocalizing, add: "You can answer me." And if necessary, also add: "Say *Yes.*"

Once the vocal response is established—and it is easily done—you may utilize this rapport to extend your control. You may ask, for example, if the subject is in a deep comfortable sleep. If the reply is negative, say: "Now I'll put you into a deeper sleep. As I count to ten, you'll relax all over and go into a very deep comfortable sleep. When I get to ten, you'll take a deep breath, relax all over and be in a deep comfortable sleep." Count slowly. Wait for the deep breath to follow the count. If it does not, add: "Take a deep breath now." Then: "You're in a deep comfortable sleep now."

Confirm the mutual vocal response by simple conversation. Tell the subject to count to ten when you say, "Count." Ask the subject his name, his address, telephone number, and other simple questions.

Confine this preliminary conversation to matters requiring a minimum of cerebration on the subject's part. Avoid questions which might stimulate the utilization of the subject's objective mind.

When ease in conversation has been established, you may extend your control further.

4. Create simple partial amnesia. Direct the subject to count to ten when you say, "Count." After the response, proceed as follows: "When I clap my hands now, the number *five* will disappear. It will be gone, completely obliterated from your mind. There will not be any such number any more. You won't be able to think of it, or to mention it."

Clap your hands deliberately and loudly three times. Then: "It's gone now. There is no such number any more.—Now count to ten when I say, *Count.* —Count."

The response should omit the number *five.* Sometimes after *four* the subject hesitates and then continues to *six.* If the response includes *five*, you should repeat the instructions and try again. Emphasize ". . . you won't be able to think of it *or to mention it . . . you will not be able to mention it . . ."* (You might also try: "It's going away, out of your mind, far away over the hills and out of your consciousness; it's gone now.")

This will generally be conducive to success in otherwise obstinate cases. Apparently an hypnotically suggested aphonia is thereby induced, resulting in forced omission of the number from the count. The fact of the omission reinforces the suggestion of mental obliteration, and upon a recount the omission is amnesic. The difference is manifested by the rapidity of the response.

When the desired response is sufficiently rapid to indicate a strong probability that the omission is amnesic, you have a good indication that a fair degree of hypnotic control has been achieved; the subject's subjective mind has accepted the suggested generalization that "there is no such number any more," and the subject's subsequent responses are circumscribed by the limits of this accepted generalization.

The degree of control thus achieved may be confirmed by requesting the subject to perform simple mathematical calculations mentally, explaining in advance that if "that number" (do not mention it by name at this point, as that would serve to recall it) or any multiple of it is involved in the calculation or in the answer, the calculation will be impossible and no answer can be given, and the subject instead of giving the answer will merely reply: "I don't know."

The question, "What is three times two?" will bring the answer, "Six." But the question, "What is seven minus two?" should result in, "I don't know." Further examples resulting in the "I don't know" response confirm the control thus far achieved.

Important: Do not forget to renormalize the subject's mental processes by saying that when you clap your hands, the number *five* will come back again; then have the subject count correctly from one to ten and perform one or two simple calculations involving the number *five*. This renormalization of the mental processes will not of itself result in any relinquishment of the control achieved.

4A. Sometimes, despite your best efforts, the subject persists in including the number *five* in his count. In that case, ask, "Why do you include the number?" The answer may be that a number cannot disappear because it is one of a series. (This is apt to occur when the subject has a strong respect for formalized mathematics.) Listen to his answer, then say: "That's right. I won't eliminate it now. Perhaps I'll do so later. In the meantime, I'll do something else." And then proceed to method 5 below.

The explanation which the subject gives for his failure to omit the number is generally interesting. In all probability it indicates that the respect in which that particular subject holds formalized mathematics is so intense that his belief in the existence of the generally accepted mathematical series approximates the proportions of an ingrained tenet. This would be the reaction of the average grade school teacher of arithmetic. Persons whose familiarity with the arabic number series is less formalized will more readily give a positive response to the suggested amnesia. So also will persons who have a more highly developed appreciation of the logical basis of mathematical thought and of the fact that the ten digit arabic number series is only an assumption in the first place.

Realizing the cause of your failure to elicit the positive response, you need have no cause for chagrin. Your reply to the subject's answer is calculated in word and tone to dispel any thought by the subject that you are distressed or disappointed. Calm assurance must be implicit in your reply. Then proceed to another reaction to regain control.

5. Repeat the hand-weighting response. If the de-

gree of control has been diminished so that the subject succeeds in raising his arm, keep repeating: "It's getting heavier, heavier, so heavy you cannot keep it up; so heavy it will fall down; it will fall down, down; it's falling down, down, back into your lap, down, down," etc. When it falls down, add: "You see it gets heavy when I say so. Things happen just the way I say they will."

5A. Create imaginary situations. For example:

(a) Suggest that the subject would probably like to take a boat ride. If he agrees, say: "All right. Now you are on the dock awaiting the boat. It's a sunny afternoon. Many people are there." Wait for the subject's facial expression to convey some slight indication of his following you; continue: "You can see the people. How many are there?" He will generally give some positive response; but if not, say: "You can see the dock clearly, can't you?—Answer me." Then, "You can see the boat, can't you?" Then, "What is the name of the boat? It's in big letters near the front." If he has difficulty in seeing it, suggest the name: "It's *Americana*. Look carefully and you'll see it. You can see it now, can't you?" And in this way lead up to the people again. "There are people on the boat. You can see them now, can't you?—How many are there?—What are they doing?" etc.—or suggest the number or activity directly.

During all of this the subject's eyes are closed. Nevertheless he responds as if his eyes were open and he were actually seeing the things you have suggested.

(b) You may similarly have the subject "take a swim" or "go to the movies" etc.

(c) Tell the subject to stand up. Then: "Now you are standing on the roof of a house, near the edge. You can look down and see the street far below. Be careful now; don't fall.—Now a wind is blowing against your back. It's getting stronger and stronger, blowing hard against your back. You can feel it blowing, can't you?" If the response is affirmative, proceed. If negative, repeat the suggestions, that it's blowing harder and harder and that the subject will feel it now, etc., until the subject admits he feels it. Then:

"It's blowing so hard, it's blowing you forward, trying to blow you off the roof. Be careful; don't let it blow you off. You're beginning to bend forward now. It's blowing so hard you can't help it—you're bending forward—don't move your feet or you'll fall off the roof. It's blowing so hard you're bending far forward now . . ." etc.

After the subject bends forward perceptibly, say: "Now it's stopping.—The wind has stopped. Stand up straight now."

Always renormalize the subject's status. For example, "Now the boat ride is over and you are back on *terra firma* with me again" would be appropriate language to terminate the illusion produced in the first illustration in 5A.

5B. Sometimes sufficient control is established during such an "excursion" so that you can proceed at once to score 21, i.e. have the subject open his eyes without affecting the trance. When the responses with the eyes closed are good, merely say: "You can open your eyes now, and you'll still stay asleep and you'll see the people on the boat. Open your eyes.— Now you still see the people, don't you?"

If the response is definitely negative, order the eyes closed at once, command relaxation and deeper sleep; do not risk losing control. If there is hesitation, say: "Look carefully. There they are. You can see them now. Point to them."—Or, "Look the other way and you'll see them. Now you see them clearly, don't you?"

Sometimes the subject admits he sees them dimly and that "they are fading away." It is well to reply: "Yes, they're walking away now. But you still see the boat (or the dock, or whatever else the subject is "standing" on) clearly, don't you?"

When the response is only mildly positive, and continued conversation with eyes open does not improve the quality of the response, order the subject to close his eyes. You may then proceed with the eyes-closed-excursions, establishing stronger control through this and other methods, before returning to the "eyes open" command.

Sometimes you may encounter moderately satisfactory responses with the eyes open without affecting the trance (score 21), even though you have failed to produce partial amnesia (score 13), and even though simple posthypnotic suggestions are not carried out (score 18). This is indicative of the highly personalized technique required in any hypnotic operation. By and large the Davis and Husband scale is a good index of the gradual degrees of trance; nevertheless, its subdivisions do not apply with mathematical precision to all individuals. The hypnotist must learn flexibility, to apply the system of graduated control as demanded by the mind and nature of the particular subject with whom he is working. Constant observation of responses and appropriate shifting of technique are required. In this phase of the work there is hardly any substitute for experience.

Should the subject awaken as the result of, or during, the eyes-open phase (or at any other time during the hypnosis), put him to sleep again quickly as described in 2B above, and then awaken him in the usual way; include posthypnotic suggestions of well-being, absence of headache, etc.

5C. If a subject fails to respond to the number amnesia, you may nevertheless succeed in producing amnesic reactions of a different nature. Just what type, depends upon the subject involved; and his explanation of why attempted number amnesia was unsuccessful is some indication of what other types of amnesia will fail, and also which ones might prove effective. Failure of the number amnesia because "it is a part of a series" might nevertheless be followed by successful suggestions that the subject does not remember where he was yesterday, or that the subject does not remember where he left the book he is reading, etc. These are of a different type: they refer to specific events which the subject recognizes could be forgotten and beyond recall.

6. Once the foregoing control, or a substantial part of it has been established, the operator may proceed with some or all of the phenomena represented through score 20 or 21 on the Davis and Husband scale; and when these have succeeded, to the rest.

It is not necessary to attempt all of them with each subject. The hypnotist who has succeeded to the point already described will learn to judge through experience when intervening steps may be omitted and more difficult phenomena attempted nevertheless.

If a difficult phenomenon is attempted and fails, drop it temporarily and fill in some or all of the previously omitted ones. The consequent gradual extension of control will be conducive to ultimate success when the more difficult phenomenon is again attempted.

Do not expect to achieve all of the possible results

in one hypnosis. Subsequent hypnoses of the same subject are generally achieved with marked increase in the rapidity of response. This is probably due to a number of factors. One of these is the subject's increased ability (resulting from experience) to co-operate with the hypnotist, which means that the subject's subjective mind will come to the fore more rapidly and with a stronger expectation of accepting the hypnotist's suggestions as true. Another factor is the hypnotist's knowledge of the subject's reactions to particular types of language and manner, as well as particular types of suggestions. Subsequent hypnoses of the same subject thus often result in positive responses to difficult degrees of suggestion previously unattainable.

The experienced hypnotist may even learn to skip step 4 above, and immediately follow the establishment of mutual conversation with phenomena of score 20. That is an individual matter. The steps here suggested are not mandatory, but they are the ones which will lead to success in most cases.

The gradation outlined in the Davis and Husband scale is worth adhering to, at least in a general way, even if not meticulously.

I shall not attempt to describe how each one of the phenomena is achieved: that is not necessary. Basically, they are all induced in the same way as those already described, that is by simple, direct suggestion. The most difficult responses (scores 25-

30) are achieved with the same simple, direct type of suggestion which induced the earlier responses, *provided* the gradation of the force of the suggestions made has been proper in degree, i.e. systematically graduated towards steadily increasing control over the subject's subjective mind.

When attempting to recapture a crucial incident or other event of the subject's early years, first secure an hypnotic depth score of at least 13 and then proceed substantially as follows: "We are now going back through the years. Where were you yesterday morning?—Now we're going further back. We're going back to the time you—(mentioning some specific occasion). Do you recall it? Describe everything that happened then.—Now you are getting younger, younger and smaller. Much younger, much smaller. You are going back to when you were twelve years old, at your twelfth birthday party. How old are you? Describe what is happening." Lead back to the crucial incident or other desired event through gradually receding memorial stages.

Certain general ideas should be kept in mind during any hypnosis.

Do not attempt to acquire control by overpowering the subject with your voice or manner. On the contrary, remember that control is achieved through directed motivation of the subject's mental processes, and that an assured, pleasantly modulated, direct conversational tone is most conducive to success.

When suggesting new generalizations to the subject, always allow time for the subjective mind to acquire them as its own before demanding a response. Speak slowly, deliberately, and distinctly. Choose your words carefully; make them simple, unambiguous; avoid all possibility of misunderstanding.

When difficulty is encountered in the establishment of control, it is often helpful to explain to the subject that success depends upon his voluntary cooperation, that you cannot hypnotize him against his will, and that if he will not strive to follow your suggestions, you may as well stop; that very young children and persons of poor mentality cannot be hypnotized, whereas intelligent people are the best subjects *because they can control their mental processes.* These statements are in fact true; they can moreover be presented to the subject in such a way that they induce the desire to cooperate.

The advisability of renormalizing by counter-suggestion any mental attitude or bodily function which you may have affected, cannot be overemphasized. Failure to do so may lead to a continuing effect of the suggestion manifesting itself at a subsequent and perhaps inopportune time.

When an unusual posthypnotic suggestion results in a positive response, it is advisable to follow the response with an explanation to the subject in the waking state that the response was posthypnotic in origin. This will prevent speculation as to the cause of his bizarre actions with possible confusion following from a misinterpretation or misconception of the cause.

The explanation may, however, be delayed until after the subject has been requested to, and attempts to, explain why he acted as he did. The positive posthypnotic response is practically always a concomitant of amnesia for the events of the trance state. The subject's explanation is therefore based, as was the response itself, upon an accepted generalization, and the explanation is merely a logical deduction therefrom.

It need hardly be added that the renormalizing suggestions and posthypnotic explanations above referred to, may be omitted in appropriate cases where the sleeping or posthypnotic suggestions are made for a therapeutic purpose.

CHAPTER TEN

Waking the Subject

T HE PROCESS of waking the subject is one of positive relinquishment of control. The relinquishment of control may be partial or complete.

It is partial when a posthypnotic suggestion remains. It is complete, either when no posthypnotic suggestion is given, or when posthypnotic suggestions which were given are subsequently eliminated by further suggestion or by full completion (acting out) of the suggestions, or when the posthypnotic suggestions which were given failed to register in the subject's mind.

The last is a rare situation; even when a posthypnotic suggestion is not acted upon by the subject,

the probability is that it has registered in his subjective mind nevertheless. (You can test this: (a) by
inquiring of him whether he remembers, or (b) by
rehypnotizing him and making the same inquiry.
Often you will receive an affirmative answer to (b)
even though it was negative to (a). "Yes" in either
case means that the posthypnotic suggestion did register, although it was not acted upon.) Therefore, in
order to avoid its having some effect at a subsequent
and possibly inopportune time, you should mention
the fact of the suggestion to your subject and state
that now it will have no effect. This can be done
even in the waking state.

Where posthypnotic suggestions have been made
with a therapeutic purpose, the relinquishment of
control in waking the subject is only partial. Even
though you relinquish all active control over the subject when you wake him, the posthypnotic suggestions you have made still control him and his thoughts
and actions. They have become accepted generalizations of his subjective mind and thus an integral part
of his mental processes.

In his waking state, the force of the posthypnotic
suggestions may at first be minimized to a degree by
the counteracting influence of the objective mind
which has now come to the fore. The subjective and
the objective act upon each other and react towards
each other. The continued control of the hypnotist
over the subject's subjective mind leads to a gradu-

ally increasing influence over the subject's objective processes as well, and thus to a remolding of his entire thought pattern. This is the basis of therapeutic hypnosis based upon implantation of suggestions in the subject's subjective mind with continuing (posthypnotic) effect.

Waking the subject with simultaneous complete relinquishment of control could be accomplished substantially as follows: state to the subject that at the count of ten he will awaken and be completely released from your influence; then count, and finish with a snap of the fingers and command, "Wake up."

This procedure is mentioned only to be condemned. It is highly inadvisable suddenly to relinquish control simultaneously with waking the subject. To do so may cause various undesirable reactions in the subject, e.g. continued drowsiness (similar to awakening from ordinary sleep, but now accounted more objectionable by the subject as an aftermath of the hypnosis), headache (sometimes caused by the sudden awakening, sometimes a result of eye strain following sight-fixation procedure in the sleep induction), or limb numbness or stiffness (resulting from incompletely removed limb catalepsy or anaesthesia), sleeplessness at night (following prolonged hypnotic rest or resulting from mental overstimulation due to the new experience). These, and other possible unpleasant after-effects may, however, be obviated as described in the following paragraphs.

Always precede the waking of the subject with a posthypnotic suggestion of euphoria, and include specific suggestions to counteract anticipated unpleasantness. A good general formula is:

"In a few moments I'm going to wake you up; and when I do, you'll be wide awake and happy; there will be no after-effects (except what I have specifically mentioned). You'll feel fine. And later when you go to sleep tonight, you'll fall asleep easily and sleep well. Now when I count to ten, you'll open your eyes and wake up, just as I told you. 1-2-3-4-5-6-7-8-9-10. Wake up.—How do you feel?"

Where a posthypnotic suggestion has been given to take effect upon a stated signal soon after the awakening, the subject may act as if not *completely* released until after the posthypnotic suggestion has been acted upon, *and* after the fact that the action was posthypnotic in nature, has been explained by the hypnotist.

In any case, individuals differ in the rapidity with which they completely awaken from hypnotic sleep, just as they do when awakening from ordinary sleep. If the subject is engaged in conversation for a few moments by the hypnotist or anyone else, the awakening process will be completed.

The popular belief that difficulty may be encountered in waking a subject is, generally speaking, unfounded. Even when it has been difficult to establish control, the relinquishment of it is simple. Fundamentally, all that is necessary is to tell the subject that in a few moments at a given signal (e.g. the count of ten) you will awaken him, and then to give the signal. It is advisable to make the signal slightly prolonged, as in the count to ten, so that the process of awakening is gradual, thus allowing time for the necessary mental shift.

Though it is possible to awaken a subject (after appropriate statement of intention so to do) with a mere snap of the fingers, or some similar sudden, momentary signal, this procedure is inadvisable. The consequent rapid mental readjustment is unnatural and may cause headache or other undesirable reaction.

In awakening the subject the hypnotist should use the same conversational tone which he has been employing all along. That is important.

Instances in which a hypnotist encounters difficulty in awakening the subject are extremely rare. There is always some specific cause for the failure, which, when understood, is quickly overcome.

The novice may be confronted by such a problem if his sudden excitement or confusion results in his changing to an excited or confused tone and manner, to the extent that the subject actually does not recognize him as the controlling medium and therefore fails to follow the directions given. A situation of this type was reported to the author. An inexperienced hypnotist, working on a good subject, obtained a strong degree of control rapidly and then suggested that the subject would open her eyes and see snakes. The subject did so, "saw" the snakes and became hysterical with fright; whereupon the hypnotist became confused and excited, and shouted further directions to her in a tone and manner which she did not recognize and therefore did not obey. The subject remained in the hypnotic state and in a state of hysterical fear of the snakes until a more experienced hypnotist was summoned to solve the problem.

After the expert had calmed the distraught tyro, he asked the latter to tell the subject, in a calm voice: "I am now going to transfer my control over you to Mr. X. The next voice you hear will be that of Mr. X and you will obey him." (Mr. X referring to the name of the experienced hypnotist.)

Thereupon Mr. X ordered the subject to close her eyes and sit down, accompanying the command with a downward push on her shoulders, and followed this with a statement that now that her eyes were closed, she could see nothing; that as he counted to ten the snakes would disappear and that when she opened her eyes, they would be gone. At the conclusion of the count she opened her eyes and the snakes were "gone." Posthypnotic amnesia was suggested and she was awakened in the usual way.

Of course, the original hypnotist, even after having "lost" control by his excited voice and manner, could have regained it easily if he had understood the cause of his difficulty. All that was necessary was for him to control his own voice and manner and to resume the conversational tone which he had employed prior to the difficulty. The subject would then have recognized her hypnotist and obeyed him.

The failure of the subject to recognize her own hypnotist upon his suddenly altering his voice and manner was due to the fact that the subject's subjective mind (to the fore in the hypnotic state) was incapable of inductive reasoning. Had she been able to reason inductively, she would have arrived at the proper generalization that he was her hypnotist from other observable particulars such as appearance, etc. In the hypnotic state, however, with only her subjective mind to the fore, she could recognize and respond only to the one particular which the subjective had already accepted as the basis of control, to wit: the hypnotist's usual conversational tone and manner.

Another possible cause of difficulty in awakening the subject, extremely rare in occurrence, may be mentioned. As the subject begins to awaken, his subjective mind is receding and his objective is in the process of coming to the fore. Where a subject has or has developed an objective antagonism to the hypnotist, the objective as it comes to the fore may possibly resent the command to awaken and cause a resistance; the subject may then not awaken on command and may either refuse to answer the hypnotist or categorically state his refusal to awaken.

This situation may be dealt with in either of two ways: (1) the hypnotist may leave the subject, who will then go into a natural sleep and awaken therefrom in due course, or (2) which is even more effective, the hypnotist may state to the subject: "All right—now you stay asleep!" This will awaken such a subject at once.

A third similar situation, extremely unusual, may arise. A hypnotized subject, after obeying some commands of the hypnotist, suddenly does not respond to any further suggestions, as if he did not hear them. Such a subject has probably fallen into a state of natural sleep. To wake him, merely shake him.

These situations are rarely encountered in practice, and are distinct exceptions to the usual reactions of the overwhelming majority of subjects.

If, after complete relinquishment of control, the subject still complains of headache, numbness or other discomfort, the condition may be quickly remedied as follows: Induce light trance quickly, emphasize posthypnotic suggestions of well-being and disappearance of the specific complaint, state that it has *now disappeared* and that its absence will continue even after you reawaken the subject. This will generally accomplish the desired result.

The extent to which a subject will remember, after awakening, the events which transpired in his hypnotic state, depends upon a number of factors. Where the hypnotist makes no specific mention of whether or not the subject will recall the events, the degree of recall depends upon the degree of trance. If the trance was light, recall is good, as dreams in a light natural sleep are remembered. The recall may be partial or complete. Sometimes the events are recalled immediately after awakening, but then fade from the memory of the subject, as ordinary dreams usually do. This fading may be accelerated if the hypnotist suggests, "You'll forget it soon, just like a dream." If the trance was deep, complete posthypnotic amnesia will probably result.

When the hypnotist gives a posthypnotic suggestion that the subject will remember everything even after awakening, then everything is recalled. On the other hand, a suggestion of posthypnotic amnesia, although it may be conducive to the suggested result, is not always effective, because if the trance was light enough, there will be recall, partial or complete, despite the contrary suggestion.

In any case, the events of a previous hypnosis are readily recalled by the same subject in subsequent hypnoses; the subjective mind (controlling memory) readily recalls its own past experiences.

Where there has been any posthypnotic amnesia, it may be removed by rehypnotizing the subject (quick, light trance is sufficient) and suggesting: "Now you recall clearly everything that happened before. When I wake you this time, you'll continue to remember everything."

CHAPTER ELEVEN

Specific Application
(Hints for the Practitioner)

---

1. *Hypnoanalysis.* Where hypnotism in conjunction with psychoanalysis (hypnoanalysis) is contemplated, begin by hypnotizing the subject at one or more sessions until, upon a given command or formula, you are able to induce a somnambulistic trance rapidly. Only then should the analysis be commenced. In this way it will be possible to throw the subject into the desired trance state quickly whenever you are ready to employ hypnosis as a part of the therapy.

Failure to establish such an hypnotic background before proceeding with the analysis leads to a two-fold disadvantage. The attempt to induce somnambulistic trance for the first time during the course of the analysis generally involves delay and procedures inimical to continuity of thought between the waking and sleeping stages. Moreover, in most instances, the use of hypnosis becomes desirable when some type of resistance has been encountered in the analysis, and this is just the point where you would have most difficulty in inducing deep trance if you have not laid the groundwork for rapid rapport in advance.

It is therefore advisable in hypnoanalysis to devote the first few sessions to an attempt to achieve hypnotic depth, and then to train the subject in some of the facets of trance procedure which may later be utilized in the therapy, e.g. posthypnotic amnesia, carrying out of various posthypnotic suggestions, dream induction, dream recall, regression, crystal gazing, automatic writing, experimentally induced disorder or conflict, etc.

2. *Hypnosis to Overcome Resistance.* The hypnoanalytic method may, however, be employed even though the preliminary analysis was commenced without any thought of subsequent hypnosis. Often prolonged analysis in the waking state results in improvement as the crucial factors are approached, but the cure remains elusive as the patient's memory refuses to regress beyond a certain point. In such cases hypnosis may then be utilized to overcome the resistance.

Several methods are possible. Induction of deep trance and continuation of analysis in this state may produce sufficient memory regression or revivification to uncover the crucial material completely with rapidity, but such instances are extremely rare. In most cases where trance is induced for the first time late in the analysis, the depth scores at first achieved are not more than 13 on the Davis and Husband scale. Even such light trance is, however, usually sufficient to produce a greater degree of recall than was accomplished in the waking state, and often results in bringing forward significant memorial factors which manifest themselves through disclosure either in the trance or during subsequent free association in the waking state. General posthypnotic suggestions of well-being, with limited specific suggestions directed to the infirmity of the particular subject, often produce an immediate improvement following the hypnotic session and create an attitude of confident expectation which sometimes in itself leads to a breakdown of the objectionable resistance.

3. *Dream Induction.* Dream induction through hypnotic suggestion is a useful method of obtaining quickly dream material confined to a particular subject matter, problem, situation or conflict. The dream may take place in the hypnotic trance or in a subsequent state of natural sleep. In either case you may thereafter guide its analysis, and this may be done with the subject either awake or in trance.

Often a failure of the subject to associate in the waking state will be followed by prompt associations of significant nature in the trance state.

When suggesting that the subject dream in the hypnotic state, you may say, "You will have a phantasy, illusion or vision like a dream about . . ." mentioning the subject matter, problem, situation or conflict. This language will cover situations in which the subject does not in fact dream upon command. In such cases his reaction to your suggestion will come within a satisfactory definition of phantasy, illusion or vision, and your hypnotic control will not be impaired thereby.

The suggestion of a dream for a subsequent ordinary sleep should be made only when the subject is in sufficiently deep trance so that there will be post-hypnotic amnesia of the fact that you are the suggesting medium. Categorically command this amnesia. Otherwise, recall of the source of the suggestion in the waking state may vitiate its effect.

It is always advisable to tell the subject that the proposed dream may or may not be in direct terms of the subject matter, problem, etc. mentioned, that it may be in terms of apparently unfamiliar but symbolical material, but that in any event he will later recall and relate it to you.

Sometimes the dream material thus produced is so intimately bound up with the crucial repressions or unconscious strivings underlying the disorder, that the dream itself is repressed and unrecalled in the waking state. In most cases, however, such repressed dreams are recalled when hypnotic trance is induced. Thus the combination of dream induction through hypnotic suggestion, and dream recall and analysis in the trance state, is a potent means of uncovering strongly repressed factors or deep unconscious strivings.

When guiding dream association or the interpretation of the associations with the subject in the trance state, it is particularly important to avoid making suggestions or interpretations which may be incorrect. The false explanation would be accepted as a true generalization by the subject's subjective mind, and would only increase the difficulty. It is, therefore, best to preface your interpretations by saying, "If it is a correct interpretation, you will understand it and accept it." In this way you induce the mental balance which enables the subject to reject an erroneous interpretation.

4. *Dream Recall.* Dream recall is always better in the hypnotic than in the waking state. The subjective mind recalls its own experiences more readily as it again comes to the fore. This is true whether the dream resulted from hypnotic suggestion or was spontaneous. In either case, the subject may have no conscious memory of it when awake and yet recall and relate it in detail when hypnotized.

5. *Automatic Writing and Crystal Gazing.* Auto-

matic writing and crystal gazing may be utilized to induce the subject to disclose memorial factors which are otherwise unobtainable because of too strong a resistance. You may inform the subject that his hand will write automatically, without his conscious awareness. The consequent production often reveals significant material. Automatic writing may take place during trance or, as the result of posthypnotic suggestion, in the subsequent waking state. In the waking state, such writing may be done in answer to a direct question. During conversation with the subject you ask an important question (e.g. "What is the cause of your fear?"), and the subject may answer orally, "I don't know," while simultaneously the hand writes a significant response.

The writing may be vague in character at first, but will become clearer as the practice progresses. Where the writing is symbolical in form or content, the subject himself may best interpret it, either through oral free association in the trance or waking state, or through further automatic writing (directed towards the task of interpretation).

If you, as an analyst, have been led to the gateway of the secret, only to find the inner sanctum barred by strong resistance, you may attempt (after producing ease in automatic writing) to say, "Your hand will now write the secret you have been keeping from me." This may be the means of producing a quick disclosure.

Crystal gazing serves a similar purpose. If a crystal is not available, a clear glass of water, or even a blank screen may be used with equal effect. The subject is put into deep trance and then told that upon opening his eyes, he should look into the crystal (or water or at the screen). Say, "You will see a picture or representation of a long-past forgotten incident, of which you have no conscious knowledge. When you see it, you will describe it to me." Here again the first revelation may require further interpretation as in the automatic writing.

A combination of regression and crystal gazing may also be utilized. After the subject has been brought back to an early level, induce crystal gazing in this regressed state. This sometimes uncovers deeply buried memories.

6. *Experimentally Induced Disorder.* Experimentally induced disorder may be used to convince the subject that his complaint is psychic only. For example, consider a case of functional paralysis of an arm, a complaint which the subject insists is genuine. You may create posthypnotic paralysis of a leg, and then remove the dysfunction in a subsequent trance, telling the subject that upon awakening he will know that the leg condition was hypnotically induced and removed. This will usually convince him that functional paralysis (i.e. a seemingly physical condition caused solely by a mental state) is not only possible, but is in fact easily produced. Such a realization is a

great stride along the road at the end of which the desired memory lies hidden.

6A. The same type of procedure is applicable to emotional situations. Neuroses resulting from repressed anxieties or conflicts may be attacked in this way. Hypnoanalysis or revelations made in the trance state may strongly indicate a particular repression as the source of the difficulty, although the subject when awake refuses to admit its existence. Where, for example, repressed hatred of a parent appears to underly the neurosis, but the subject when awake rejects the possibility of any such emotion, hypnosis may be used to suggest, "When I awaken you, I will ask you to look at the picture of a man in a book. When you do, your reaction to the picture will be the same as your unconscious attitude towards your father, although you will not remember that I was the one who suggested this." If the subsequent reaction is unpleasant or antagonistic, i.e. one of emotional conflict, your suspicions are confirmed. Note that you did not suggest what the subject's reactions would be, whether favorable or antagonistic; the reaction is the subject's own.

Give the subject ample opportunity to observe his own reaction, without yet revealing to him the cause thereof. Then rehypnotize him, recall to him the fact that you suggested the similarity of attitude, and state that upon reawakening, he will remember everything that happened during both trances and in the intervening waking state. This will aid in producing a quick conscious realization of the repressed conflict.

7. *Memory Regression.* Memory regression is best achieved with the subject in somnambulistic trance. When the subject refuses to divulge the desired incidents through this method, it is helpful to suggest that he will reveal the troublesome memories or events a part at a time. This sometimes results in the installment production of important material which you may then proceed to organize into appropriate unit form. Such a procedure may be used not only in connection with the usual analysis or hypnoanalysis, but with crystal gazing and automatic writing as well.

8. *Symptom Alleviation.* Aside from his specific complaint, the average patient will usually report one or more symptoms of what may be termed the neurotic syndrome—headache, inability to sleep, excessive use of barbiturates, hypersensitivity to noise, inability to concentrate, etc. These factors, although often only incidental to the major cause of the underlying difficulty, are of extreme importance to the patient. They may in most instances be alleviated or removed quickly by direct hypnotic suggestion in the preliminary sessions. For example, the patient may be enabled, through simple posthypnotic suggestion, to fall asleep at night, without taking his accustomed barbiturates, when he counts mentally

to five. The successful response is generally appreciated by the patient to a degree out of all proportion to its fundamental significance, but this appreciation will be extremely helpful in rapidly establishing a confidence and rapport which will be conducive to continued cooperation. This fosters the psychological transference. In some cases it may prevent an otherwise indecisive patient from discontinuing treatment before the ultimate desideratum is achieved.

It should be remembered, however, that unless the underlying difficulty is attacked, symptom removal or alleviation by hypnotic suggestion alone may be of temporary duration only.

9. *Recall of Trance Events.* Occasionally subjects, upon awakening from hypnotic sleep, will maintain that they were not hypnotized because they are able to recall what transpired during the trance state. In some cases this belief tends to weaken the prestige element necessary for successful therapy. This difficulty may be obviated by explaining to the subject (in advance, or even after the awakening) that the fact that he may remember what happened is not necessarily an indication of failure of hypnosis, for such recall is merely in the nature of a remembered dream. You may refer to the attainment of a physical reaction (arm rigidity, for example) as proof that hypnotic control was achieved.

10. *Privacy.* The patient's solicitous relative who wishes to be present to "watch the hypnotism" is a

certain stumbling block on the road to successful
treatment. More often than not, the patient, his
statements to the contrary notwithstanding, prefers
no witness (especially a close relative) to what he
may say when hypnotized. In many cases relegating
the relative to the waiting room will be the first step
towards achieving successful results.

11. *Resistance to Hypnosis.* Where the subject re-
sists hypnosis, it is often possible to overcome his
negative attitude by explaining something about the
nature of the process. Try to ascertain the cause of
his resistance and then dispel it. Make him realize
that the hypnotic process is not one in which you
dominate him, but rather one in which he himself
reorganizes his mental processes subject to your aid
and direction. Convince him that you cannot control
him against his will, but only with his consent, and
that the extent of your success depends upon the
degree of his active cooperation. Sometimes a subject's resistance results from a conscious or subconscious fear that you will probe into secret depths
which he prefers to keep buried. Such resistance
may be overcome through assurance that he will not
be forced to reply to any questions which he does
not desire to answer.

12. *Insusceptible Subjects.* For the patient who
fails to respond to all attempts to hypnotize him, or
who never goes beyond light trance, it may be helpful to explain that deep hypnotic sleep is not essen-

tial. Bramwell, in *Hypnotism, Its History, Practice and Theory,* reports the case of a sailor who complained of inability to walk following an accident at sea (the ship sank carrying him down, and a subsequent explosion blew him to the surface). Bramwell writes:

"On May 8th, 1902, he was sent to me by Dr. Roome of Southsea. The patient told me that he had never known what sickness was until his accident. He now complained of nothing but his inability to walk: his general health was excellent, and he never felt ill or depressed. He was powerfully built and strong in the arms, but the muscles of the lower extremities were markedly wasted and flabby, and the pulse weak. Reflexes much exaggerated: the slightest touch over the patella produced a violent convulsive kick. Further, any muscular stimulus, particularly if unexpected, produced an immediate response. For example, if his foot touched an inequality in the bedclothes, he would be almost thrown out of bed by the violence of the muscular start. . . .

"His walking was still limited to moving a little about his room, with the aid of a chair. Anything beyond this was followed by a fall. At first the exciting cause was mainly emotional: he fell if any one came near him. Later, he fell if he attempted to walk with the assistance of another person: if he encountered the slightest inequality in the ground he tumbled, and dragged his companion with him. This did not occur because his legs failed him; his fall seemed always due to a distorted or exaggerated reflex. The slightest unexpected stimulus to the soles of the feet was followed by a convulsive response, when he fell rigidly and violently on the back of his head. Beyond this I could discover nothing abnormal. There was no paralysis, no loss of consciousness, and no alterations in sensation other than those just described.

"I began hypnotic treatment on May 8th, and continued it five times a week until July 24th, 1902, when the patient returned to Portsmouth. *Hypnosis, in the sense in which I understand it, was never induced. Apparently nothing was done beyond making 'curative suggestions,' while the patient rested quietly in an armchair: he never even became drowsy.* Despite this, the result was striking. In a week he could cross his room; and, after the first month, he spent hours at a time walking about the streets and parks. He even went into crowds without fear or tremor, and saw the various military reviews, etc., which were held at that time."

The italics are mine. I have quoted this at some length because in a few cases where patients could not be hypnotized, I found that reading this passage to them was conducive to cooperation and moderate success with suggestions made in a passive waking state.

13. *Use of Another Hypnotist.* Where you believe that hypnosis may be beneficial in the course of treatment, but cannot induce it yourself, or prefer not to, you may have someone else hypnotize the

subject in your presence. The other hypnotist may then ask the appropriate questions or make the desired suggestions in consonance with your wishes, or may direct the hypnotized subject to listen to or converse with you, thus permitting you to take a more direct control of the questions asked and suggestions made.

14. *Co-Hypnotist.* In some instances it may prove helpful to have the hypnosis induced by another person, even though you are personally conversant with hypnotic methods. This is suggested for a case in which you have not established advance hypnotic rapport with the subject and are now contemplating the use of trance to overcome or circumvent a resistance which has developed during the analysis. In such a situation a hypnotist other than yourself may well be able to induce deep trance more quickly than you. Control could then be shifted to you, after which you might arrange, through posthypnotic suggestion, to reinduce the trance yourself at subsequent sessions.

CHAPTER TWELVE

Representative Cases

1. JAMES BRAID, in his *Neurypnology*, reports that he successfully applied hypnotism to the relief and cure of many ailments including imperfect vision, incipient deafness, impaired sense of smell, abnormalities in the sense of touch, nervous headache, olfactory hallucinations, loss of voice, and paralysis. One woman, who complained, "My baby is fourteen months old, and I have scarcely any milk," was hypnotized by Braid who records: "Although her child was fourteen months old, and before being hypnotized she complained of having had very little milk, these hypnotic processes had given such a stimulus to the mammae, that this lady was enabled to continue to suckle her

child from an overflowing breast for six months longer."

2. Robert M. Lindner, in *Rebel Without a Cause,* reports the cure of a psychopathic criminal through the use of hypnoanalysis. Harold, the subject of the report, was the victim of psychically founded antisocial tendencies. He was a criminal, in the legal sense. Psychiatrists who had examined him described him as suffering from ". . . psychopathic personality complicated by social difficulties arising from the condition of the boy's eyes." One reported him ". . . cowardly, unreliable, and a schemer." The last examiner, before Lindner, concluded ". . . unless someone is able to psychoanalyze and reconstruct his personality from about three years of age on, the boy will continue on his career of crime and, because of his violent impulses, will become a more and more dangerous criminal."

Lindner employed a combination of Freudian free-association and hypnotism. Preliminary psychoanalytic conversation in the waking state was followed by the use of hypnosis to evoke deeply-rooted repressed memories which apparently constituted the bases of Harold's abnormalities. Using free-association as the pathway to the hidden past, and hypnosis as the key to the door of memory, Lindner opened the recesses of Harold's mind. He uncovered the repressed and buried memories which had caused the psychic maladjustment, and in doing so achieved a remarkable result. ". . . the patient was 'cured' in the sense of alteration of style of life, and imbued with a real ability to live with his particular ocular symptom. The alteration was based on what some psychologists call 'insight,' on a real understanding of the past and a reorientation of attitudes and aims. Harold today sees better, feels better, behaves better. Individuals who know him and work with him comment on his radically altered pattern of behavior. Gone is that sneering sullenness, that arrogant aggression, that Storm-Trooper mentality, that disregard for the rights and feelings of others. He knows that he was a psychopath: he knows why he was a psychopath: he knows that he needs to be a psychopath no more. . . ."

In the case of Lindner's Harold, the crucial memory proved to be an incident which had occurred when he was about two years of age. He had unexpectedly awakened and witnessed an act of intercourse between his parents. His infantile mind translated it into a brutal physical attack by his father upon his mother. He associated this impression with a fancied resemblance, of daydream origin, between his father and a ferocious animal. A deep unconscious hatred of his father became firmly implanted. As he grew older, this unreasoning hatred of, and consequent rebellion against, the "authority" of his home, was carried over into his attitude towards all authority in society. He became a rebel, not knowing why. But when the true cause of his rebellious spirit was revealed through hypnoanalysis, he realized that he had been a "rebel without a cause," and he was cured.

3. Lewis R. Wolberg, in his *Hypnoanalysis*, reports the case of Johan R. In this case a psychosis occurred when Johan was 42 years of age. He became tense and fearful, and said that life was meaningless. He lost interest in his appearance and refused to take food. He heard the voice of God chiding him for his sins. He continually lamented his plight and the hopelessness of his situation.

Wolberg used a large variety of hypnotic procedures to foster and supplement the psychoanalytic process, including dream induction, automatic writing, hypnotic drawing, experimental conflict, mirror gazing, and regression. By a skilfull combination of these hypnotic techniques he succeeded in integrating Johan's schizophrenic personality—and accomplished his results in a period of only four months.

4. L. F. Beck reports an interesting case in "Hypnotic Identification of an Amnesia Victim," published in the *British Journal of Medical Psychology*. The subject's fugue had resulted from psychological conflict pertaining to his relationship with his wife and child, involving a desire not to return to his previous environment. Although deep hypnosis was quickly achieved, the subject failed to answer when asked his name, and merely showed signs of great agitation. When automatic writing was suggested, he wrote

"Marian" and later the surname "Kingsley," which turned out to be the name of his wife. When confronted with these in the waking state, he remembered the names and most of his previous associations with them, and this in turn led to recall of his own identity.

5. Sergei Rachmaninoff, the pianist and composer, in his *Recollections,* discloses some unusual circumstances surrounding the composition of his Concerto for Piano and Orchestra in C minor, No. 2, Opus 18. He had been suffering from severe apathy, despondence and depression, and was unable to work. His family proposed that he consult a Dr. N. Dahl, who was a pioneer in the field of suggestion and autosuggestion. Rachmaninoff visited him from January to April of 1900. The composer's own report is as follows:

"My relations had told Dr. Dahl that he must at all costs cure me of my apathetic condition and achieve such results that I would again begin to compose. Dahl had asked what manner of composition they desired and received the answer, 'A Concerto for pianoforte,' for this I had promised to the people in London and had given it up in despair. Consequently I heard the same hypnotic formula repeated day after day while I lay half asleep in an armchair in Dahl's study, 'You will begin to write your Concerto . . . You will work with great facility . . . The Concerto will be of an excellent quality . . .' . . . Although it may sound incredible, this cure really helped me. Already at the beginning of the summer I began again to compose. The material grew in bulk, and new musical ideas began to stir within me—far more than I needed for my Concerto. By the autumn I had finished two movements of the Concerto—the Andante and the Finale . . . The two movements of the Concerto (Op. 18) I played during the same autumn . . . The two movements of my Concerto had a gratifying success . . .

"I felt that Dr. Dahl's treatment had strengthened my nervous system to a miraculous degree. Out of gratitude I dedicated my second Concerto to him."

6. Mrs. K. was in her late forties, married, and the mother of two children. Her complaint was a severely impaired power to vocalize.

A little over three years ago, she began to experience trouble in speaking. During the first year her difficulty increased considerably until it finally became necessary for her to exert great effort in order to utter the simplest word. Her sentences were labored forth, a word at a time. The effort involved caused severe pain in her side, near the diaphragm. Her syndrome included severe headaches, inability to sleep (except with the aid of barbiturates), and marked depression. In the last two years she had forsaken all social contacts, because she shrank from the curiosity of those who observed her condition. She left her home only to shop for the family's needs, and was compelled to use a written list as her sole means of communication with the tradespeople.

A number of physicians whose aid she had enlisted had attempted to treat her with pills, injections, and throat-spraying—all without avail.

Examination by a neurologist revealed no organic defect whatsoever. A diagnosis of hysterical dysphonia was made, and hypnoanalysis was prescribed.

I saw the patient twice a week for a total of twenty-one visits. Each session was devoted partly to discussion and analysis in the waking state, and partly to hypnotic procedures. The insomnia, the headaches, and the side pain were completely eliminated through direct hypnotic suggestion within the first four sessions. A combination of regression, dream induction, and experimentally induced disorder was used to uncover and explain the underlying cause of her neurosis.

The patient revealed that her husband had frequently come home intoxicated. That, to her, was one of the worst things a man could do. Over a number of years she had developed a growing fear of his home-coming. When he opened the door, she would gaze at him in terror, and this terror became habitual. The gasping breath and her strangulated voice resulted. Her pitiable condition aroused her husband's sympathy, and finally, in accordance with her often expressed wish, he foreswore whiskey for beer.

She was content with his drinking beer, as that did not intoxicate him. Her home life was thus satisfactory and, as she said, if only she could regain her voice, she would be completely happy again. But if he ever went back to drinking whiskey, ". . . that would be the worst thing in the world": she would break up her home, leave him, and take the children with her back to her native Scotland.

It was at this point that the nature of the psychoanalytic process was explained to her. She thereupon volunteered the information that ever since she had lost her voice, she had acquired a very sweet taste in her throat; it was pleasant, and was with her always. She associated this taste with the heather of Scotland, where she had spent her childhood, a very happy one.

It was now clear that the strangulated voice had been the means of separating her husband from whiskey. Unconsciously she had maintained the weapon which gave her mastery of the situation, and prevented the "worst thing in the world" from happening, even at the cost of continued suffering; suffering which, great as it was, was still not "the worst thing in the world."

When this was pointed out to her, her symptoms began to disappear. She sees and talks with friends and neighbors, and enjoys using her newly regained voice. The only complaint she reported at the last session was from the vegetable-vendor: she had given him an argument about the quality of his produce!

I need hardly add that analysis, without the aid of hypnosis, would have taken a very much longer time. Indeed, in view of the speech difficulty, analysis alone might have been almost impossible. The hypnosis permitted a quick alleviation of the speech difficulty, sufficient to allow for freer discussion; it hastened transference, and made possible the special techniques which led directly to uncovering the cause of the neurosis, as well as its appreciation by the patient.

7. An example of the use of hypnosis to induce hypermnesia is the case of Miss W. She wished to locate an important business letter that had somehow been lost. She reported that the last time she recalled seeing it was in her office in New York about a year before our conference, and that she thought she had filed it among certain records, but that she had now searched for it in vain.

Under hypnosis, in answer to specific questions, she related when she had first received the letter, several occasions when she had handled it, and finally the last time she had seen it. That, she stated, was about nine months past in the guest room of her aunt's house in Boston, while she was packing her valise to leave. Had she put it into the valise? "No." Had she ever seen it after that? "No."

I awakened her and informed her that she had left

the letter in the guest room in Boston. She was dubious, but said that she would check with her aunt.

Some weeks thereafter she reported to me that inquiry had confirmed what she had revealed during hypnosis. The letter had been left in Boston, and fortunately her aunt had kept it for her.

8. Miss H., aged 16, required a blood test for which a large quantity of blood had to be drawn from her vein by insertion of a long needle attached to a syringe. It was essential for the purposes of the test that she remain calm as the blood was being drawn. Drug-anaesthesia could not be employed, as it might affect the blood stream. The patient, however, was unusually sensitive to, and fearful of pain. The sight of the long needle at the end of the syringe threw her into a paroxysm of fear which resulted in her leaving the hospital without having submitted a blood specimen.

This happened on several occasions. It seemed impossible to secure the cooperation of the patient.

At this point a psychological approach was suggested. I hypnotized her and suggested anaesthesia at the count of eight, first upon my counting and then upon her counting alone. This was followed by posthypnotic suggestion of carryover into the waking state, with the result that thereafter she was able, while awake, to anaesthetize her arm upon her own count to eight; and she accomplished this, even though she counted mentally.

Two days later she reported to the physician at the hospital, counted mentally, said *ready* out loud, and accepted the needle without pain.

9. The case of Miss C. demonstrates the speed and ease with which results may sometimes be attained. She was in the habit of smoking about two packs of cigarettes a day, and desired to reduce the amount without strain. At the first session she went into deep sleep. I suggested that cigarettes would taste bitter, and received a positive reaction in both the sleeping and waking states. I told her she would smoke not more than ten cigarettes a day until our next session.

There was no next session. She telephoned to break the appointment, and some weeks later informed me that since she was now smoking only ten cigarettes a day, there was no necessity for further hypnosis.

10. Mrs. J. was an attractive woman, whose complaint was that she felt sure everyone knew her teeth were false. Actually, it was not at all evident that she did wear artificial dentures, but she lived in a constant state of mortification in the belief that the defect was obvious. After three hypnotic sessions, in which only simple posthypnotic suggestion was employed, she was entirely relieved of her embarrassment.

Bibliography

ADLER, D. L.: The Experimental Production of Repression. *Proceedings of the Eighth Annual Meeting of Topological Psychologists*, 27-36, 1940.

ALEXANDER, F. et. al.: Psychogenic Factors in Bronchial Asthma. *Psychosomatic Medicine Monographs*, 1941.

ALEXANDER, F. and WILSON, G. W.: Quantitative Dream Studies. *Psychoanalytic Quarterly*, 4: 371-407, 1935.

AVELING, F. and HARGREAVES, H. L.: Suggestibility With and Without Prestige in Children. *British Journal of Psychology*, 12: 52-75, 1921.

BABINSKI, J.: My Conceptions of Hysteria and Hypnotism. *Alienist and Neurologist*, 19: 1, 1908.

BARRY, H. JR. et al.: Studies in Personality. *Human Biology*, 3: 1-36, 1931.

BARTLETT, M. R.: Relation of Suggestibility to Other Personality Traits. *Journal of General Psychology*, 15: 191-196, 1936.

BARTLETT, M. R.: Suggestibility in Psychopathic Individuals. *Journal of General Psychology*, 14: 241-247, 1936.

BASS, M. J.: Differentiation of Hypnotic Trance from Normal Sleep. *Journal of Experimental Psychology*, 14: 382-399, 1931.

BAUDOUIN, C.: *Suggestion and Autosuggestion*. New York, Dodd, Mead & Co., 1922.

BECHTEREW, W. V.: What is Hypnosis? *Journal of Abnormal Psychology*, 1: 18-25, 1906.

BECK, L. F.: Hypnotic Identification of an Amnesia Victim, *British Journal of Medical Psychology*, 16: 36-42, 1938.

BECK, L. F.: Relationships Between Waking Suggestibility and Hypnotic Susceptibility. *Psychological Bulletin*, 33: 747, 1936.

BEHANON, K. T.: *Yoga, A Scientific Evaluation*. New York, Macmillian, 1937.

BERGMAN, J. S. et al.: Rorschach Exploration of Consecutive Hypnotic Age Level Regressions. *Psychosomatic Medicine*, 20-28, Jan.-Feb. 1947.

BERNHEIM, H.: *Suggestive Therapeutics*. New York, London Book Company, 1947.

BINET, A. and FERE, C.: *Animal Magnetism*. New York, D. Appleton & Co., 1888.

BIRNIE, C. R.: Anorexia Nervosa Treated by Hypnosis. *Lancet*, 2: 1331-1332, Dec. 5, 1936.

BRAID, J.: *Neurypnology*. London, G. Redway, 1899.

BRAMWELL, J. M.: *Hypnotism, Its History, Practice and Theory*. Philadelphia, J. B. Lippincott Co., 1903.

BRENMAN, M. and GILL, M.: *Hypnotherapy*. New York, International Universities Press, 1947.

BRENMAN, M.: Self-Starvation and Compulsive Hopping with Paradoxical Reaction to Hypnosis. *American Journal of Orthopsychiatry*, 9: 65-75, 1945.

BRENMAN, M. and KNIGHT, R. P.: Hypnotherapy for Mental Illness in the Aged. *Bulletin of Menninger Clinic*, 7: 5-6, 188-198, 1943.

BRENMAN, M. and REICHARD, S.: Use of the Rorschach Test in the Prediction of Hypnotizability. *Bulletin of Menninger Clinic*, 7: 5-6, 183-187, 1943.

BRENMAN, M.: Experiments in the Hypnotic Production of Anti-Social and Self-Injurious Behavior. *Psychiatry*, 5: 49-61, 1942.

BREUER, J. and FREUD, S.: *Studies in Hysteria*. Nervous and Mental Disease Monograph Series, 1936.

BRICKNER, R. M. and KUBIE, L. S.: A Miniature Psychotic Storm Produced by Super-Ego Conflict over Simple Post-hypnotic Suggestion. *Psychoanalytic Quarterly,* 5: 467-487, 1936.

BROOKS, C. H.: *The Practice of Autosuggestion by the Method of Émile Coué.* New York, Dodd, Mead & Co., 1922.

BROSIN, H. W.: Panic States and Their Treatment. *American Journal of Psychiatry,* 100: 58, 1943.

BROWN, H.: *Advanced Suggestion.* New York, William Wood & Co., 1919.

BROWN, W.: *Psychology and Psychotherapy.* London, Edward Arnold & Co., 1934.

BROWN, W.: *Suggestion and Mental Analysis.* New York, Doran, 1922.

BROWN, W.: Hypnosis, Suggestibility and Progressive Relaxation. *British Journal of Psychology,* 28: 396-411, 1938.

BROWN, W.: Hypnosis, Suggestion and Dissociation. *British Medical Journal,* June 14, 1919.

BROWN, W.: The Treatment of Cases of Shell-shock in Advanced Neurological Center. *Lancet,* 197-200, August 7, 1918.

BUCKLE, H. T.: *History of Civilization in England,* New York, Hearst's International Library Co., 1913. (Cf. Vol. II, pages 324 *et seq.* where the distinction between the inductive and deductive methods and their respective influences upon historical development are discussed.)

BURNETT, C. T.: Splitting the Mind. *Psychological Monograph,* 34: No. 2, 1925.

CARLILL, H.: Hypnotism. *Lancet,* 1: 61-66, January 5, 1935.

CHARCOT, J. M.: Oeuvres Completes, *Metallotherapie et Hypnotisme.* Tome IX, Paris, Bourneville et E. Brissaud, 1890.

CHARCOT, J. M.: *Lectures on the Diseases of the Nervous System.* London, The New Sydenham Society, 1877–1889.

CHARCOT, J. M.: *Poliklinische Vortrage.* Leipzig and Vienna, F. Deuticke.

CONNELLAN, P. S.: The Treatment of Repressed Memories by

Hypnotism. *Bristol Medical-Chirurgical Journal,* 43: 209-216, 1926.

CONNELLY, E.: Uses of Hypnosis in Psychotherapy. *New Orleans Medical and Surgical Journal,* 88: 627-632, 1936.

COPELAND, C. L. and KITCHING, E. H.: Hypnosis in Mental Hospital Practice. *Journal of Mental Science,* 83: 316-329, 1937.

COUÉ, E.: *How to Practice Suggestion and Autosuggestion.* American Library Service, 1923.

COUÉ, E.: *Self-Mastery Through Conscious Autosuggestion.* New York, American Library Service, 1922.

DAVIS, L. W. and HUSBAND, R. W.: A Study of Hypnotic Susceptibility in Relation to Personality Traits. *Journal of Abnormal and Social Psychology,* 26: 175-182, 1931.

DAVIS, R. C. and KANTOR, J. R.: Skin Resistance During Hypnotic State. *Journal of General Psychology,* 13: 62-81, 1935.

DEJERINE, J. and GAUCHLER, E.: *Psychoneuroses and Psychotherapy.* Philadelphia, J. B. Lippincott, 1913.

DESSOIR, M.: *Bibliography of Modern Hypnotism.* Berlin, C. Dunckner, 1888.

DIETERLE, R. R. and KOCH, E. J.: Experimental Induction of Infantile Behavior in Major Hysteria. *Journal of Nervous and Mental Diseases,* 86: 688-710, 1937.

DONLEY, J. E.: The Clinical Use of Hypnoidization in the Treatment of Some Functional Psychoses. *Journal of Abnormal Psychology,* 3: 148-160, 1908–1909.

DORCUS, R. M.: Modification by Suggestion of Some Vestibular and Visual Responses. *American Journal of Psychology,* 49: 82-87, 1937.

DOUPE, J. et. al.: Vasomotor Reactions in the Hypnotic State. *Journal of Neurology and Psychiatry,* 2: 106, 1939.

DREUGER, R. G.: The Influence of Repetition and Disuse Upon Rate of Hypnotization. *Journal of Experimental Psychology,* 14: 260-269, 1931.

DUBOIS, P.: *Psychoneuroses and Their Psychic Treatment.* Bern, Francke, 1905.

DUNLAP, K.: *Habits, Their Making and Unmaking*. New York, Liveright, 1933.

DuPOTET DE SENNEVOY, J.: *Magnetism and Magic*. London, G. Allen & Unwin, 1927.

DYNES, J. B.: An Experimental Study in Hypnotic Anaesthesia. *Journal of Abnormal and Social Psychology*, 27: 87, 1932.

EBERT, E. C.: Hypnosis in Psychogenic Amblyopia. *United States Navy Medical Bulletin*, 29: 248, July 1931.

ERICKSON, M. H. and HILL, L.: Unconscious Mental Activity in Hypnosis. *Psychoanalytic Quarterly*, 13: 60-78, January 1944.

ERICKSON, M. H.: Concerning the Nature and Character of Posthypnotic Behavior. *Journal of General Psychology*, 24: 95-133, 1941.

ERICKSON, M. H.: The Successful Treatment of a Case of Acute Hysterical Depression by a Return Under Hypnosis to a Critical Phase of Childhood. *Psychoanalytic Quarterly*, 10: 583-609, October 1941.

ERICKSON, M. H. and KUBIE, L. S.: The Translation of the Cryptic Automatic Writing of One Subject by Another in a Trance-Like Dissociated State. *Psychoanalytic Quarterly*, 9: 51-63, 1940.

ERICKSON, M. H.: The Induction of Color Blindness by a Technique of Hypnotic Suggestion. *Journal of General Psychology*, 20, 61-89, 1939.

ERICKSON, M. H.: The Applications of Hypnosis to Psychiatry. *Medical Record*, 150: 60-65, 1939.

ERICKSON, M. H. and KUBIE, L. S.: The Permanent Relief of an Obsessional Phobia by Means of Communication with an Unsuspected Dual Personality. *Psychoanalytic Quarterly*, 8: 471-509, October 1939.

ERICKSON, M. H.: A Study of Clinical and Experimental Findings on Hypnotic Deafness. *Journal of General Psychology*, 19: 127-150 and 151-167, 1938.

ERICKSON, M. H.: The Use of Automatic Drawing in the Interpretation and Relief of a State of Acute Obsessional Depression. *Psychoanalytic Quarterly,* 7: 443-466, 1938.

ERICKSON, M. H.: Development of Apparent Unconsciousness During Hypnotic Reliving of a Traumatic Experience. *Archives of Neurology and Psychiatry,* 38: 1282-1288, 1937.

ERICKSON, M. H.: The Experimental Demonstration of Unconscious Mentation by Automatic Writing. *Psychoanalytic Quarterly,* 6: 513, 1937.

ERICKSON, M. H.: A Study of Experimental Neurosis Hypnotically Induced in a Case of Ejaculatio Praecox. *British Journal of Medical Psychology,* 15: 34-50, 1935.

ERICKSON, M. H.: The Investigation of a Specific Amnesia. *British Journal of Medical Psychology,* 13: 143-150, 1933,

ESTABROOKS, G. H.: A Standardized Hypnotic Technique Dictated to a Victrola Record. *American Journal of Psychology,* 42: 115-116, 1930.

ESTRIN, J.: Hypnosis as Supportive Symptomatic Treatment in Skin Diseases. *Urologic and Cutaneous Review,* 45: 337-338, May 1941.

FARBER, L. H. and FISCHER, G.: An Experimental Approach to Dream Psychology Through the Use of Hypnosis. *Psychoanalytic Quarterly,* 12: 202-216, 1943.

FERENCZI, S.: *Theory and Technique of Psychoanalysis.* New York, Boni & Liveright, 1927.

FERENCZI, S. et al.: *Psycho-analysis and the War Neuroses.* London, International Psycho-analytical Press, 1921.

FERENCZI, S.: *Sex in Psychoanalysis.* Boston, Richard G. Badger, 1916.

FISCHER, C.: Hypnosis in Treatment of Neuroses Due to War and to Other Causes. *War Medicine,* 4: 565-576, December 1943.

FOREL, A.: *Hypnotism.* New York, Allied Publications, 1927.

FRAZER, J. G.: *The Golden Bough.* New York, The Macmillan Co., 1931. (Cf. pages 204 *et seq.* in which instances of death resulting from suggestion alone are related.)

FREUD, S.: *The Question of Lay Analysis.* New York, W. W. Norton & Co., Inc., 1950.

FREUD, S.: *An Outline of Psychoanalysis.* New York, W. W. Norton & Co., Inc., 1949.

FREUD, S.: *An Autobiographical Study.* London, Hogarth Press, 1948.

FREUD, S.: *The Ego and the Id.* London, Hogarth Press, 1947.

FREUD, S.: *The Basic Writings of Sigmund Freud.* Modern Library, Random House, 1938.

FREUD, S.: *Interpretation of Dreams.* New York, Macmillan Co., 1933.

FREUD, S.: *Group Psychology and the Analysis of the Ego.* London, International Psycho-analytical Press, 1922.

FRIEDLANDER, J. W. and SARBIN, T. R.: The Depth of Hypnosis. *Journal of Abnormal and Social Psychology,* 33: 453-475, 1938.

FROESCHELS, E.: Pathology and Therapy of Stuttering. *The Nervous Child,* 2: 158-160, 1943.

FROMM-REICHMANN, F.: Transference Problems in Schizophrenia. *Psychoanalytic Quarterly,* 8: 412, 1939.

GERRISH, F.: The Therapeutic Value of Hypnotic Suggestion. *Journal of Abnormal Psychology,* 4: 99, 1909.

GILL, M. M. and BRENMAN, M.: Treatment of a Case of Anxiety Hysteria by an Hypnotic Technique. *Bulletin of Menninger Clinic,* 7: 5-6, 163-171, 1943.

GOLDWYN, J.: The Effect of Hypnosis on Basal Metabolism. *Archives of Internal Medicine,* 45: 109-114, 1930.

GOLDWYN, J.: Hypnoidalization. *Journal of Abnormal Psychology,* 24: 170-185, 1929.

GRINKER, R. R. and SPIEGEL, J. P.: *War Neuroses in North Africa.* New York, Joshia Macy, Jr. Foundation, 1943.

GRINKER, R. R. and SPIEGEL, J. P.: Brief Psychotherapy in War Neuroses. *Psychosomatic Medicine,* 6: 125, 1944.

GURNEY, E.: Recent Experiments in Hypnotism. *Proceedings of the Society for Psychical Research,* 5: 3, 1888.

HADFIELD, J. A.: *The Neuroses in War.* New York, Macmillan Co., 1940.

HADFIELD, J. A.: War Neuroses. *British Medical Journal*, 1: 320, March 1942.

HADFIELD, J. A.: The Reliability of Infant Memories. *British Journal of Medical Psychology*, 13: 87-111, 1928.

HADFIELD, J. A.: Chapter on Hypnotism in *Functional Nerve Disease* edited by H. C. Miller. London, Hodder & Stoughton, Ltd., 1920.

HARRIMAN, P. L.: The Experimental Production of Some Phenomena Related to the Multiple Personality. *Journal of Abnormal and Social Psychology*, 37: 244-255, 1942.

HART, B.: *Psychopathology*. New York, Macmillan Co., 1927.

HART, H. H.: Hypnosis in Psychiatric Clinics. *Journal of Nervous and Mental Diseases*, 74: 598-609, 1931.

HEYER, G.: *Hypnosis and Hypnotherapy*. London, C. W. Daniel Co., 1931.

HIBLER, F. W.: An Experimental Investigation of Negative After Images of Hallucinated Colors in Hypnosis. *Journal of Experimental Psychology*, 27: 45-57, 1940.

HILGER, W.: *Hypnosis and Suggestion*. New York, The Rebman Co., 1921.

HOLLANDER, B.: *Methods and Uses of Hypnosis and Self-Hypnosis*. London, George Allen & Unwin, Ltd., 1935.

HOLLANDER, B.: *Hypnotism and Suggestion in Daily Life, Education and Medical Practice*. New York, G. P. Putnam's Sons, 1910.

HORSLEY, J. S.: *Narco-Analysis*. London, Oxford University Press, 1943.

HUDSON, T. J.: *The Law of Psychic Phenomena*. Chicago, A. C. McClurg & Co., 1899.

HULL, C. L.: *Hypnosis and Suggestibility*. New York, D. Appleton-Century, 1933.

HUNT, J. M.: *Personality and the Behavior Disorders*, New York, Ronald Press, 1944.

HURST, A. F. and SYMNS, J. L. M.: The Rapid Cure of Hysterical Symptoms in Soldiers. *Lancet*, 2: 139-141, August 3, 1918.

HUSE, B.: Does the Hypnotic Trance Favor the Recall of

Faint Memories? *Journal of Experimental Psychology*, 13: 519-529, 1930.

HUSTON, P. E. et. al.: A Study of Hypnotically Induced Complexes by Means of the Luria Technique. *Journal of General Psychology*, 11: 65-97, 1934.

IMBERT-GOUBEYRE, A.: *L'hypnotisme et la Stigmatisation*. Paris, Bloud et Barral, 1899.

JANET, P.: *Psychological Healing*. New York, Macmillian Co., 1925.

JANET, P.: *Principles of Psychotherapy*. New York, Macmillan Co., 1924.

JANET, P.: *The Major Symptoms of Hysteria*. New York, Macmillian Co., 1907.

JANET, P.: *The Mental State of Hystericals*. New York, G. P. Putnam's Sons, 1901.

JENNESS, A.: Chapter on Hypnotism in *Personality and the Behavior Disorders* edited by J. M. Hunt, pages 446-502. New York, The Ronald Press, 1944.

JENNESS, A. and DAHMS, H.: Change of Auditory Threshold During Reverie as Related to Hypnotizability. *Journal of General Psychology*, 17: 167-170, 1937.

JENNESS, A. and WIBLE, C. L.: Respiration and Heart Action in Sleep and Hypnosis. *Journal of General Psychology*, 16: 197-222, 1937.

JENNNESS, A.: Facilitation of Response to Suggestion by Response to Previous Suggestion of a Different Type. *Journal of Experimental Psychology*, 16: 55-82, 1933.

JONES, E.: The Nature of Auto-suggestion. *British Journal of Medical Psychology*, 3: 206-212, 1923.

JONES, E.: The Action of Suggestion in Psychotherapy. *Journal of Abnormal Psychology*, 5: 217-254, 1910.

KALZ, F.: Psychological Factors in Skin Diseases. *Canadian Medical Association Journal*, 53: 247, 1945.

KANZER, M. G.: The Therapeutic Use of Dreams Induced by Hypnotic Suggestion. *Psychoanalytic Quarterly*, 14: 313, 1945.

KARDINER, A. and SPIEGEL, H.: *War Stress and Neurotic Ill-ness.* New York, Paul B. Hoeber, Inc., 1947.

KARDINER, A.: *The Traumatic Neuroses of War.* Psychoso-matic Medicine Monograph III. Washington, National Re-search Council, 1941.

KELLER, D. H.: A Psychoanalytic Cure of Hysteria. Spring-field, Ill. *Institutional Quarterly,* 8: 78-82, 1917.

KELLOGG, E. R.: Duration of the Effects of Posthypnotic Sug-gestion. *Journal of Experimental Psychology,* 12: 502-514, 1929.

KENNEDY, F.: War Neurosis As It Is Related to Psychoso-matic Medicine. *New York State Journal of Medicine,* 45: 21, 2285-2290, 1945.

KENNEDY, F.: The Inter-Relationship of Mind and Body. *Journal of the Mount Sinai Hospital,* IX: 4, 607-616, 1942.

KIER, G.: An Experiment in Mental Testing Under Hypnosis. *Journal of Mental Science,* 91: 346-352, 1945.

KIERNAN, J. G.: Hypnotism in American Psychiatry Fifty Years Ago. *American Journal of Insanity,* 51: 336-354, 1894–1895.

KLEIN, D. B.: The Experimental Production of Dreams Dur-ing Hypnosis. *University of Texas Bulletin,* 3009: 1-71, 1930.

KRAFT-EBING, R.: *An Experimental Study in the Domain of Hypnosis.* New York, G. P. Putnam's Sons, 1889.

KRAINES, S. H.: *The Therapy of the Neuroses and Psychoses.* Philadelphia, Lea & Febiger, 1941.

KROGER, W. S. and FREED, S. C.: The Psychosomatic Treat-ment of Functional Dysmenorrhea by Hypnosis. *American Journal of Obstetrics and Gynecology,* 817-822, December 1943.

KUBIE, L. S. and MARGOLIN, S.: The Process of Hypnotism and the Nature of the Hypnotic State. *American Journal of Psychiatry,* 100: 611-622, March 1944.

KUBIE, L. S.: Manual of Emergency Treatment for Acute War Neuroses. *War Medicine,* 4, 6: 582-589, December 1943.

KUBIE, L. S.: Use of Induced Hypnagogic Reveries in the Recovery of Repressed Amnesic Data. *Bulletin of Menninger Clinic,* 7, 5-6: 172-182, Sept.-Nov. 1943.

KUBIE, L. S. and MARGOLIN, S.: A Physiological Method for the Induction of States of Partial Sleep, etc. *Transactions American Neurological Association,* 1942.

KUHN, L. and RUSSO, S.: *Modern Hypnosis.* New York, Psychological Library, 1947.

LECRON, L. M. and BORDEAUX, J.: *Hypnotism Today.* New York, Grune & Stratton, 1947.

LESHAN, L.: The Breaking of a Habit by Suggestion During Sleep. *Journal of Abnormal and Social Psychology,* 37: 406-408, 1942.

LEUBA, C.: The Use of Hypnosis for Controlling Variables in Psychological Experiments. *Journal of Abnormal and Social Psychology,* 36: 271-274, 1941.

LEVBARG, J. J.: Hypnosis: a Potent Therapy in Medicine. *New York Physician,* 14: 18, 1940.

LEVBARG, J. J.: Hypnosis—Potent Therapy for Certain Disorders of Voice and Speech. *Archives of Otolaryngology,* 30: 206-211, August 1939.

LEVINE, M.: *Psychotherapy in Medical Practice.* New York, Macmillian Co., 1942.

LINDNER, R. M.: *Rebel Without a Cause.* New York, Grune & Stratton, 1944.

LIVINGOOD, F. G.: Hypnosis as an Aid to Adjustment. *Journal of Psychology,* 12: 203-207, 1941.

LLOYD, B. L.: *Hypnotism in the Treatment of Disease.* London, Bale & Danielsson, 1934.

LOOMIS, A. L. and HARVEY, E. N.: Brain Potentials During Hypnosis. *Science,* 83: 239-241, 1936.

LUNDHOLM, H. and LOWENBACH, H.: Hypnosis and the Alpha Activity of the Electroencephalogram. *Character and Personality,* 11, 2: 145-149, 1942.

LUNDHOLM, H.: An Experimental Study of Functional Anaesthesias as Induced by Suggestion in Hypnosis. *Journal of Abnormal and Social Psychology,* 23: 337-355, 1928.

LURIA, A. R.: *The Nature of Human Conflicts.* New York, Liveright Pub. Corp., 1932.

MARKS, R. W.: *The Story of Hypnotism.* New York, Prentice-Hall, 1947.

MASSERMAN, J.: *Behavior and Neurosis.* Chicago, University of Chicago Press, 1943.

MCDOUGALL, W.: *Outline of Abnormal Psychology.* New York, Chas. Scribner's Sons, 1926.

MCDOUGALL, W.: Four Cases of "Regression" in Soldiers. *Journal of Abnormal Psychology,* 15: 136-156, 1920.

MILLER, E.: *The Neuroses in War.* New York, Macmillan Co., 1940.

MILLER, H. C.: *Functional Nerve Disease.* London, Oxford University Press, 1920.

MILLER, H. C.: *Hypnotism and Disease.* Boston, The Gorham Press, 1912.

MITCHELL, M. B.: Retroactive Inhibition and Hypnosis: *Journal of General Psychology,* 7: 343-359, 1932.

MOLL, A.: *Hypnotism.* New York, C. Scribner's Sons, 1902.

MOORE, W. E.: Hypnosis in a System of Therapy for Stutterers. *Journal of Speech Disorders,* 11: 117-122, 1946.

MORGAN, J. J. B.: Hypnosis with Direct Psychoanalytic Statement and Suggestion in the Treatment of a Psychoneurotic of Low Intelligence. *Journal of Abnormal Psychology,* 19: 160-164, 1924.

MORGAN, J. J. B.: The Nature of Suggestibility. *Psychological Review,* 31: 6, 1924.

MOTT, F. W.: *War Neuroses and Shell Shock.* New York, Oxford University Press, 1919.

MUHL, A. M.: Automatic Writing Combined with Crystal Gazing as a Means of Recalling Forgotten Incidents. *Journal of Abnormal Psychology,* 19: 264-273, 1924.

MUHL, A. M.: Automatic Writing in Determining Conflict and Early Childhood Repressions. *Journal of Abnormal Psychology,* 18: 1-32, 1923.

MUNSTERBERG, H.: *Psychology, General and Applied.* New York, D. Appleton & Co., 1915.

MUNSTERBERG, H.: *Psychotherapy*. New York, Moffat, Yard & Co., 1909.

MUNSTERBERG, H.: *Psychology and Life*. Boston, Houghton Mifflin Co., 1899.

MURRAY, H.: *Explorations in Personality*. New York, Oxford University Press, 1939.

MYERS, C. S.: The Revival of Emotional Memories and Its Therapeutic Value. *British Journal of Medical Psychology*, 1: 26, October 1920.

NEUSTETTER, W. L.: *Early Treatment of Nervous and Mental Disorders*. London, Churchill, 1940.

NYGARD, J. W.: Cerebral Circulation Prevailing During Sleep and Hypnosis. *Psychological Bulletin*, 34: 727, 1937.

OBERNDORF, C. P.: Consideration of Results with Psychoanalytic Therapy. *American Journal of Psychiatry*, 99: 377, 1942.

PATTIE, F. A.: The Production of Blisters by Hypnotic Suggestion. *Journal of Abnormal and Social Psychology*, 36: 62-72, 1941.

PATTIE, F. A.: The Genuiness of Hypnotically Produced Anaesthesia on the Skin. *American Journal of Psychology*, 49: 435-443, 1937.

PAVLOV, I. P.: Inhibition, Hypnosis and Sleep. *British Medical Journal*, 256-267, 1923.

PAVLOV, I. P.: The Identity of Inhibition with Sleep and Hypnosis. *Scientific Monthly*, 17: 603-608, 1923.

PIERCE, F.: *Mobilizing the Mid-brain*. New York, Dutton, 1924.

PLATONOW, K. I.: On the Objective Proof of the Experimental Personality Age Regression. *Journal of General Psychology*, 9: 190-209, 1933.

PRINCE, M.: *Clinical and Experimental Studies in Personality*. Second edition. Edited by A. A. Roback. Cambridge, Sci-Arts, 1939.

PRINCE, M.: *The Unconscious*. New York, Macmillan Co., 1929.

PRINCE, M. et al.: *Psychotherapeutics.* Boston, The Gorham Press, 1912.

PRINCE, M.: *The Dissociation of a Personality.* Second edition. New York, Longmans, Green & Co., 1908.

PRINCE, M.: Automatic Writing Combined with Crystal Gazing. *Journal of Abnormal Psychology,* 20: 34, 1925–1926.

PRINCE, M. and PUTNAM, J.: A Clinical Study of a Case of Phobia. *Journal of Abnormal Psychology,* 7: 259-292, 1912.

QUACKENBOS, J. D.: *Hypnotic Therapeutics in Theory and Practice.* New York, Harper, 1908.

RADO, S.: The Economic Principle in Psycho-analytic Technique. *International Journal of Psychoanalysis,* 6: 35-44, 1935.

RAEDER, O. J.: Hypnosis and Allied Forms of Suggestion in Practical Psychotherapy. *American Journal of Psychiatry,* 13: 67-76, 1933.

RAPAPORT, D.: *Emotions and Memory.* Baltimore, The Williams & Wilkins Co., 1942.

RAPAPORT, D.: Freudian Mechanisms and Frustration Experiments. *Psychoanalytic Quarterly,* 9: 503-511, 1942.

RIVERS, W. H. R.: *Instinct and the Unconscious.* Cambridge, University Press, 1922.

ROGERSON, C. H.: Narcoanalysis with Nitrous Oxide. *British Medical Journal,* 1: 811-812, June 17, 1944.

ROSENOW, C.: Meaningful Behavior in Hypnosis. *American Journal of Psychology,* 40: 205-235, 1928.

ROSENZWEIG, S. and SARASON, S.: An Experimental Study of the Triadic Hypothesis. *Character and Personality,* 11: 2, 1-19, December 1942.

Ross, T. A.: *The Common Neuroses.* Baltimore, Wm. Wood & Co., 1937.

Ross, T. A.: *Prognosis in the Neuroses.* Cambridge, University Press, 1936.

Ross, T. A.: The Prevention of Relapse of Hysterial Manifestitations. *Lancet,* 516-517, October 19, 1918.

ROTHENBERG, S.: Theories of Hypnosis and Its Use. *New York State Journal of Medicine,* 28: 372-378, 1928.

ROWLAND, L. W.: Will Hypnotized Persons Try to Harm Themselves and Others? *Journal of Abnormal and Social Psychology,* 34: 114-117, 1939.

SALTER, A.: *What Is Hypnosis.* New York, Richard R. Smith, 1944.

SALTER, A.: Three Techniques of Autohypnosis. *Journal of General Psychology,* 24: 423-438, 1941.

SARBIN, T. R. and MADOW, L. W.: Predicting the Depth of Hypnosis by Means of the Rorschach Test. *American Journal of Orthopsychiatry,* 12: 2, 268-270, April 1942.

SARBIN, T. R.: Rorschach Patterns Under Hypnosis. *American Journal of Orthopsychiatry,* 9: 315-318, 1939.

SARGENT, W. and FRASER, R.: Inducing Light Hypnosis by Hyperventilation. *Lancet,* 235: 778, 1938.

SATOW, L.: *Hypnotism and Suggestion.* New York, Dodd, Mead & Co., 1923.

SCHILDER, P.: *Psychotherapy.* New York, W. W. Norton & Co., 1938.

SCHILDER, P. and KAUDERS, O.: *Hypnosis.* Nervous and Mental Disease Monograph Series, No. 46, 1927.

SCHWARTZ, O.: *Psychotherapy and Psychogenesis of Corporeal Symptoms.* Vienna, Springer, 1925.

SCOTT, F. G. L.: Ten Consecutive Cases Treated by Hypnotism. London, *Guys Hospital Report,* 52: 114-119, 1913.

SCOTT, H. D.: Hypnosis and the Conditioned Reflex. *Journal of General Psychology,* 4: 113-130, 1930.

SEARS, R. R.: Survey of Objective Studies of Psychoanalytic Concepts. *Social Science Research Council Bulletin,* No. 51, New York, 1942.

SEARS, R. R.: An Experimental Study of Hypnotic Anaesthesia. *Journal of Experimental Psychology,* 15: 1-22, 1932.

SEXTUS, C.: *Hypnotism.* New York, H. M. Caldwell Co., 1893.

SHARP, A. A.: An Experimental Test of Freud's Doctrine of the Relation of Hedonic Tone to Memory Survival. *Journal of Experimental Psychology,* 22: 395-418, 1938.

SIDIS, B.: *Nervous Ills: Their Cause and Cure.* Boston, Richard G. Badger, 1922.

SIDIS, B.: *Foundations of Normal and Abnormal Psychology.* Boston, Richard G. Badger, 1914.

SIDIS, B.: *An Experimental Study of Sleep.* Boston, Richard G. Badger, 1909.

SIDIS, B. and GOODHART, S. P.: *Multiple Personality.* New York, D. Appleton & Co., 1905.

SIDIS, B.: *Psychopathological Researches.* New York, G. E. Stechert, 1902.

SIDIS, B.: *The Psychology of Suggestion.* New York, D. Appleton-Century, 1898.

SIDIS, B.: The Value of the Method of Hypnoidization in the Diagnosis and Treatment of Psychopathic Disorders. *Medical Times of New York,* XLVII, 245-250, 1919.

SMITH, G. M.: A Phobia Originating Before the Age of Three—Cured With the Aid of Hypnotic Recall. *Character and Personality,* 5: 331-337, 1937.

SOUTHARD, E. E.: *Shell-Shock and Other Neuropsychiatric Problems.* Boston, W. M. Leonard, 1919.

SPEYER, N. and STOKVIS, B.: The Psychoanalytic Factor in Hypnosis. *British Journal of Medical Psychology,* 17: 217-222, 1938.

STALNAKER, J. M. and RIDDLE, E. E.: The Effect of Hypnosis on Long-delayed Recall. *Journal of General Psychology,* 6: 429-449, 1932.

STEKEL, W.: *Psychoanalysis and Suggestion Therapy.* London, Kegan Paul, 1923.

STEWART, K. R.: Color Blindness and Tone Deafness Restored to Health During Psychotherapeutic Treatment Using Dream Analysis. *Journal of Nervous and Mental Diseases,* 93: 716-718, 1941.

TAPLIN, A. B.: *Hypnotism and Treatment by Suggestion.* Liverpool, Littlebury Bros., 1928.

TAPLIN, A. B.: *Hypnotic Suggestion and Psycho-Therapeutics.* London, Simpkin, Marshall, Hamilton, Kent & Co., 1918.

TAYLOR, W. S.: Behaviour Under Hypnoanalysis and the Mechanism of the Neurosis. *Journal of Abnormal Psychology*, 18: 107-124, 1923.

TAYLOR, W. S.: A Hypnoanalytic Study of Two Cases of War Neurosis. *Journal of Abnormal Psychology*, 16: 344-355, 1921–1922.

TOMBLESON, J. B.: An Account of 20 Cases Treated by Hypnotic Suggestion. London, *Journal Royal Army Medical Corps*, 340-346, 1917.

TOMKINS, S. S.: *Contemporary Psychopathology*. Cambridge, Harvard University Press, 1943.

TRAVIS, R. C.: A Study of the Effect of Hypnosis on a Case of Dissociation Precipitated by Migraine. *American Journal of Psychology*, 36: 207, 1925.

TROTTER, R. H.: Neurasthenic and Hysterical Cases in General Military Hospitals. *Lancet*, 703, November 23, 1918.

TUCKEY, C. L.: *Treatment by Hypnotism and Suggestion or Psychotherapeutics*. London, Bailliere, Tindall & Cox, 1921.

UTARD, W.: The Hypnotic State. Calcutta, *New Review*, 29-44, January 1942.

VAN PASSEN, P.: *Days of Our Years*. Garden City, New York, Garden City Publishing Co., Inc., 1940. (Cf. pages 246 *et seq.* in which a weird incident is described, the explanation of which becomes clear in the light of the Theory of Psychic Relative Exclusion applied to autohypnosis.)

VITOZ, R.: *Treatment of Neurasthenia by Means of Brain Control*. London, Longmans, Green, 1913.

VON REISEMANN, O.: *Rachmaninoff's Recollections*. London, George Allen & Unwin, 1934. (Cf. pages 111-113.)

WALDEN, E. C.: A Plethysmographic Study of the Vascular Conditions During Hypnotic Sleep. *American Journal of Physiology*, 4: 124-161, 1900.

WALSH, J. J.: *Psychotherapy*. New York, Appleton Century, 1913.

WELCH, L.: The Space and Time of Induced Hypnotic Dreams. *Journal of Psychology*, 1: 171-178, 1936.

WELLS, W. R.: Experiments in the Hypnotic Production of Crime. *Journal of Psychology,* 11: 63-102, 1941.

WELLS, W. R.: Ability to Resist Artificially Induced Dissociation. *Journal of Abnormal and Social Psychology,* 35: 261-272, 1940.

WELLS, W. R.: The Extent and Duration of Posthypnotic Amnesia. *Journal of Psychology,* 9: 137-151, 1940.

WELLS, W. R.: Experiments in Waking Hypnosis for Instructional Purposes. *Journal of Abnormal and Social Psychology,* 18: 389-404, 1924.

WETTERSTRAND, O. G.: *Hypnotism and Its Application to Practical Medicine.* New York, G. P. Putnam's Sons, 1902.

WHITE, M. M.: Evidence from Hypnosis of Inhibition as a Factor in Recall. *Psychological Bulletin,* 32: 689-690, 1935.

WHITE, M. M.: The Physical and Mental Traits of Individuals Susceptible to Hypnosis. *Journal of Abnormal and Social Psychology,* 25: 293-298, 1930.

WHITE, R. W. and SHEVACH, B. S.: Hypnosis and the Concept of Disassociation. *Journal of Abnormal and Social Psychology,* 37: 3, 309-328, July 1942.

WHITE, R. W.: A Preface to the Theory of Hypnotism. *Journal of Abnormal and Social Psychology,* 36: 477-505, 1941.

WHITE, R. W.: An Analysis of Motivation in Hypnosis. *Journal of General Psychology,* 24: 145-162, 1941.

WHITE, R. W. et al.: Hypnotic Hypermnesia for Recently Learned Material. *Journal of Abnormal and Social Psychology,* 35: 88-103, 1940.

WHITE, R. W.: Hypnosis Test. Pages 453-461 in Murray's *Explorations in Personality,* New York, Oxford University Press, 1938.

WHITE, R. W.: Prediction of Hypnotic Susceptibility from a Knowledge of Subject's Attitudes. *Journal of Psychology,* 3: 265-277, 1937.

WHITE, R. W.: Two Types of Hypnotic Trance and Their Personality Correlates. *Journal of Psychology,* 3: 279-289, 1937.

WILLIAMS, G. W.: A Comparative Study of Voluntary and Hypnotic Catalepsy. *American Journal of Psychology*, 42: 83-95, 1930.

WILLIAMS, G. W.: Suggestibility in the Normal and Hypnotic States. *Archives of Psychology*, 19, No. 122, 1930.

WILLIAMS, G. W.: The Effect of Hypnosis on Muscular Fatigue. *Journal of Abnormal and Social Psychology*, 24: 318-329, 1929.

WINGFIELD, H. E.: *An Introduction to the Study of Hypnotism, Experimental and Therapeutic.* London, Bailliere, Tindall & Cox, 1920.

WINN, R. B.: *Scientific Hypnotism.* Boston, Christopher, 1939.

WITTKOWER, E.: Studies on the Influence of Emotions on the Functions of Organs. *Journal of Mental Science*, 81: 533, 1935.

WOLBERG, L. R.: *Medical Hypnosis.* New York, Grune & Stratton, 1948.

WOLBERG, L. R.: *Hypnoanalysis.* New York, Grune & Stratton, 1945.

WOLBERG, L. R.: Hypnotic Experiments in Psychosomatic Medicine. *Psychosomatic Medicine*, 9: 337-342, 1947.

WOLBERG, L. R.: A Mechanism of Hysteria Elucidated During Hypnosis. *Psychoanalytic Quarterly*, 14: 1945.

WOLBERG, L. R.: Phallic Elements in Primitive, Ancient, and Modern Thinking. *Psychiatric Quarterly*, 18: 278-297, 1944.

WOOKEY, E. E.: Uses and Limitations of Hypnosis in Dental Treatment. *British Dental Journal*, 65: 562-568, 1938.

YEALLAND, L. R.: *Hysterical Disorders of Warfare.* New York, Macmillan Co., 1918.

YELLOWLEES, H.: *A Manual of Psychotherapy.* London, A. & C. Black, Ltd., 1923.

YOUNG, P. C.: Experimental Hypnotism. *Psychological Bulletin*, 38: 92-104, 1941.

YOUNG, P. C.: Hypnotic Regression—Fact or Artifact? *Journal of Abnormal and Social Psychology*, 35: 273-278, 1940.

YOUNG, P. C.: Suggestion as Indirection. *Journal of Abnormal and Social Psychology*, 26: 1, 69-90, April 1931.

YOUNG, P. C.: Is Rapport an Essential Characteristic of Hypnosis? *Journal of Abnormal and Social Psychology*, 22: 130-139, 1927.

YOUNG, P. C.: A General Review of the Literature on Hypnotism. *Psychological Bulletin*, 24: 540-560, 1927.

ZILBOORG, G.: *History of Medical Psychology*. New York, W. W. Norton & Co., 1941.

Index

Free Catalog
of New Age & Occult Books From Carol Publishing Group

For over 30 years, the Citadel Library of the Mystic Arts has been hailed as America's definitive line of works on Occult Sciences and Personalities, Magic, Demonology, Spiritism, Mysticism, Natural Health, Psychic Sciences, Witchcraft, Metaphysics, and Esoterica.

<u>Selected titles include:</u> • The Alexander Technique • Amulets and Talismans • Apparitions and Survival of Death • Astral Projection • At the Heart of Darkness • The Bedside Book of Death • Beyond the Light: What Isn't Being Said About the Near-Death Experience • Blackstone's Tricks Anyone Can Do • The Book of Ceremonial Magic • The Book of the Dead • Buddha and the Gospel of Buddhism • Candlelight Spells • The Candle Magick Workbook • The Case for Reincarnation • The Complete Guide to Alternative Cancer Therapies • The Concise Lexicon of the Occult • Cosmic Consciousness • Daily Meditations for Dieters • Deceptions and Myths of the Bible • Dracula Book of Great Horror Stories • Egyptian Magic • Egyptian Religion • An Encyclopedia of Occultism • Encyclopedia of Signs, Omens and Superstitions • The Fairy-Faith in Celtic Countries • The Grim Reaper's Book of Days • Gypsy Sorcery and Fortune Telling • A History of Secret Societies • The History of Witchcraft • The Hollow Earth • The Holy Kabbalah • How To Embalm Your Mother-In-Law • How to Improve Your Psychic Power • How to Interpret Your Dreams From A - Z • How To Make Amulets, Charms and Talismans • Hypnosis • I Ching Book of Changes • The Kabbalah • The Lost Language of Symbolism, Vols. 1 & 2 • Lighting the Seventh Fire: The Science, Healing and Spiritual Ways of the Native American • The Magick of Candle Burning • The Magus • The Mark of the Beast • Meaning in Dreams and Dreaming • The Modern Witch's Book of Home Remedies • The Modern Witch's Dreambook • The Modern Witch's Spellbook, 1 & 2 • Moon Madness • Not of This World • Numerology • Our Earth, Our Cure • Out-of-the-Body Experiences • The Pictorial Key to the Tarot • Principles of Light and Color • The Roots of Healing: A Woman's Book of Herbs • Satanism • Satanism and Witchcraft • The Secrets of Ancient Witchcraft • The Secrets of Love Magick • Shouting at the Wolf • Silent Witness: The True Story of a Psychic Detective • Stranger Than Science • Strangest of All • Strange World • Study and Practice of Astral Projection • The Symbolism of Color • The Talisman Magick Workbook • Tarot Cards • Teachings of Tibetan Yoga • A Treasury of Witchcraft • The Vampire • The Werewolf of Paris • Where the Ghosts Are • Wicca Craft • Wicca Spellbook • Window To the Past • Witchcraft • Witch-Doctor's Apprentice • You Are All Sanpaku • Zen Macrobiotic Cooking

Ask for these New Age and Occult books at your bookstore. To order direct or to request a brochure, call 1-800-447-BOOK or send your name and address to Carol Publishing Group, 120 Enterprise Avenue, Dept 1119, Secaucus, NJ 07094.

Books subject to availability